BORN A WOMAN

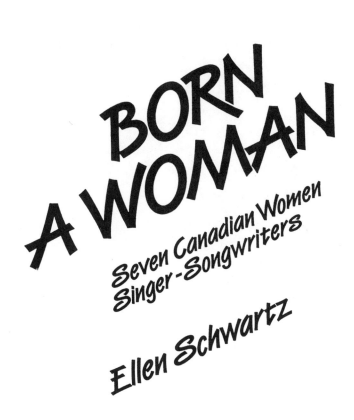

BORN A WOMAN

Seven Canadian Women
Singer-Songwriters

Ellen Schwartz

POLESTAR
BOOK PUBLISHERS

for Bill

Published by
Polestar Press Ltd., R.R. 1, Winlaw, B.C., V0G 2J0   604-226-7670

Published with the assistance of the Canada Council and the Government of British Columbia, through the Ministry of Tourism, Recreation and Culture.

Canadian Cataloguing in Publication Data
Schwartz, Ellen, 1949 —
Born a woman
Discography: p.
ISBN 0-919591-25-6
1. Women musicians — Canada — Biography. I. Title.
ML82.S32 1988   780'.92'2   C88-091283-9

Cover and book design by Jim Brennan.

Printed in Canada.

Acknowledgements

The author wishes to thank the following for their assistance and encouragement:

Kris Anderson
Bob Bossin
Valdine Ciwko
Gary Cristall
Markandrew Cardiff
Brookes Diamond
Ruth Dworin
Leslie Fiddler
Richard Flohil
Joella Foulds
Rosalie Goldstein
Estelle Klein
Joan Miller
Paul Mills
Mitch Podolak
Diane Potvin
Les Siemieniuk
Hilda and Phil Thomas
Frances Wasserlein

Special thanks to Gary Cristall and the staff of the Vancouver Folk Music Festival.

This book was written with the assistance of a Non-fiction Writing Grant from the Canada Council.
Special thanks to Claudine Guay.

Born a Woman is the title of Rita MacNeil's first album, released in 1975. The publisher gratefully acknowledges permission for its use.

Contents

Introduction

Imagine two great roads intersecting. One is folk music, specifically the North American folk music revival of the '60s and '70s. The other is the women's movement.

Folk music has traditionally been played on portable, handmade instruments—guitar, banjo, fiddle, harmonica, sticks, spoons, drums. And it has always been topical, concerning itself with the joys, troubles and aspirations of common people—as opposed to the more lofty concerns of the nobility. In seventeenth century Canada, for example, broadsides—songs written on one side of a sheet of paper, often satires about contemporary political issues— flourished in Ontario and Quebec. In the Maritimes, folk songs exposed the hardships of the seafaring life. In the '30s and '40s, political songwriting reflected the development of the Communist Party and the bitter and often violent struggles of the labour union movement. Ban the bomb, civil rights, the Vietnam War—these issues sparked the revival of topical songwriting in the '60s and '70s.

Later in the '70s, folk music faded. Acoustic sounds gave way to rock and roll, while socially-conscious lyrics yielded to a growing sense of disillusionment, apathy and conservatism and were replaced by words with no political content.

The women's movement of the 1960s was not a new development, but a resurgence of earlier struggles. Like generations before them, women of the '60s and '70s recognized the injustices they suffered in every field from health care to employment, and they organized to work for legislative and social change. What was different was that they were more vocal and built a broader base of support than previous women's rights activists.

Along with political action, the feminist movement produced something that might be called "women's vision." Underlying this vision was the assumption that women's point of view, their way of perceiving and relating to the world, was different from, and as valid as, that of men. Women's vision was holistic and ecologically aware. It championed open, cooperative relations between people.

The intersection of folk music and the women's movement resulted in a form of culture known as "women's music." (More on terminology later.) Feminists found the folk music style — typically solo voice accompanied by guitar or piano — a suitable vehicle for their messages. Later they moved beyond the acoustic sound, but they retained the social consciousness characteristic of folk music. (Indeed, as the '70s progressed and disco became the musical rage, women's music was one of the few bodies of music — along with music generated by the gay rights movement, the native rights movement and others — that continued to address political concerns.) In a sense, the creators of women's music picked up where the "folkies" left off.

Unapologetically taking a female point of view, women wrote songs exploring issues long ignored. In "Woman's World," for example, Sylvia Tyson described the circumscribed domain of womanhood:

> Woman's world, cooking and babies
> Little girls with knowing eyes
> Woman's world, caught in a circle
> Smaller than truth and bigger than lies.

Women wrote songs protesting women's exclusion from traditionally male occupations and positions of authority. Women wrote songs exposing their treatment as sexual objects: *"To be born a woman, you quickly learn/Your body will be their first concern,"* Rita MacNeil said in "Born a Woman." From sexual object it was a short distance to sexual victim: women began to speak out in their music about sexual violence, wife battering and child abuse. Through their songs, women demanded political, economic and social changes and expressed their unique vision.

The women's movement supported the women musicians by providing a receptive audience eager to hear music that matched its experience. At women's conferences, rallies, demonstrations and celebrations, musicians had the opportunity to perform at a time when the general public was not willing or ready to listen sympathetically. In some cases the women's political circuit provided a living for singer-songwriters who otherwise wouldn't have been able to survive singing their own music.

As with most political-cultural movements, women's music at first focused inward. Themes were women-centred, and so was the audience that listened to it and championed it. But gradually the songwriters expanded their approach. While still writing from a woman's experience and with a woman's sensibility, they began to address more universal themes. Over and over the women in this book have said, "I *am* a feminist, but I'm not a feminist songwriter. My music isn't just about and for women. It's for everyone." As the concerns of women songwriters widened, so did their audiences.

Audiences developed differently, though, in Canada and the United States. In the States the mainstream folk festivals didn't expand to include genres such as women's music. Instead a system of separate music festivals emerged to accommodate women's music, gay music, country music, reggae, and so on, and for the most part there was little crossover between these festivals and the mainstream events. For example, Bonnie Raitt would appear at the Philadelphia Folk Festival, where she might perform a few tunes with feminist content, but a feminist performer like Holly Near would not be invited to Philadelphia and would instead play at the Michigan Women's Music Festival.

In Canada the folk festivals were always integrated. From its start in 1961, the Mariposa Folk Festival, Canada's first large festival, featured both men and women performers, including feminist musicians, in its programming. Other Canadian folk festivals — in Winnipeg, Vancouver, Calgary, Edmonton, Owen Sound, and so on — followed Mariposa's model. Perhaps Canada's small population couldn't sustain a large number of differently focused events; perhaps it was a result of Canada's tradition of social democracy and tolerance. Whatever the reasons, the development has served Canadian women singer-songwriters well, giving them an opportunity to present their music to large, mixed audiences, not just members of their sub-group.

In this country, women's music has naturally been influenced by Canadian factors. The French-English question affects the work of people close to that issue, such as Marie-Lynn Hammond and Lucie Blue Tremblay. Regional identification shows up both thematically and musically, from Rita MacNeil's songs inspired by Cape Breton to Connie Kaldor's country-flavoured tunes about the prairies. Canadian music often conveys a sense of place, of the vastness of the landscape and the isolation of its people: Heather Bishop's "The Northlands" is one example. Perhaps most important, the music expresses, if only on a subtle level, an awareness of unique Canadian history and values, distinct from those of other nations. To be Canadian means something to the women in this book.

When women's music emerged in the '60s, songwriters used folk-style ballads as their main form of expression. Since that time, popular music has evolved from acoustic to electric to electronic sounds, and women's music has followed these trends. Women musicians now compose rock and roll, jazz, country, new wave music — whatever genre suits the song. Most of the women in this book play acoustic guitar and/or piano, but they perform with rock-style backup and use synthesizers and other high-tech equipment on their albums.

Whether the style of their music is folk or pop, the intent remains the same: To write with conviction about their own experiences. To explore issues they care about. To write from the heart.

Before we investigate the musicians, a word on semantics. What do we call this music? Folk music? Women's music? Country music? Contemporary music? Feminist music? Acoustic music? Pop-rock? Folk-rock? Aaargghh!

The phrase folk music is a troublesome one. Pete Seeger said, "A song isn't a folk song unless it's been passed down from one generation to another without being written down." The Canadian Encyclopedia agrees, defining folk music as "the music of ordinary people: songs and tunes that are passed on from one to another by ear rather than by print... They are sung or played for pleasure rather than for profit, and usually the composer is unknown." On the other hand, Big Bill Broonzy, an American blues musician, said, "All songs is folk songs. I never heard a horse sing." Certainly the music under consideration in this book falls between these two definitions. So is it folk music?

Yes and no. Everyone who uses the phrase means something different by it. Folk purists reserve the label for traditional music: to them "Barbara Allen" is a folk song, while "If I Had a Hammer" is not. In the '30s and '40s union organizers called their music "people's music" and themselves "folksingers."

In the '60s the music of Bob Dylan, Joan Baez, Tom Paxton and Joni Mitchell was called folk music because it was played on acoustic instruments (thus connecting it to traditional music) and it conveyed a message, usually political. But in a strict sense it wasn't folk music. It was contemporary, acoustic, topical music—and the acoustic aspect ended when Bob Dylan went electric at the Newport Folk Festival. The music of the women in this book is not necessarily acoustic, nor does it conform to the ballad format that we usually associate with folk songs. It is not traditional music, although it may draw on regional and ethnic influences. So it isn't really folk music.

What about "women's music" or "feminist music"? The women in this book naturally write from a woman's point of view. They all describe themselves as feminists. Often they compose songs around issues and experiences of special interest to women. But—and here is the big but—not all of their songs are about women's issues. Like any other kind of music, much of their material explores universal themes.

And—and this is an important and—they are not the only ones writing songs about issues of special interest to women. In recent years many men have been writing songs about "women's issues": sexual violence, child abuse, equal rights, parenthood, and so on. Male songwriters have been expressing their feelings in a way that has traditionally been considered the domain of women artists. Murray McLauchlan's "Louisa Can't Feed Another Child" is a "women's song." So is Bruce Cockburn's "Peggy's Kitchen Wall." The songs of Connie Kaldor have more in common with those of Roy Forbes than with those of Madonna.

When women musicians began to address issues of sexual equality in their music, the phrase women's music may have been useful as a way to indicate their intent and their commitment, as a way to inform people that their concerns were as valid as any others. But now to call their music women's music is, I think, to limit it, and to exclude much good material by men that arises from the same source of commitment. It is women's music, yes, but more than that it is people's music. It is not only for feminists, not only for lesbians, not only for people of a particular political persuasion. It is for men, women and children—anyone who wants to listen to music that cares.

If it isn't folk music and it isn't women's music, what is it? The answer is that there is no phrase that is perfectly accurate or adequate. In this book I reluctantly use the terms folk music and women's music. I hope readers will understand them in a general, inclusive sense. Perhaps that's the point: What really matters is not the label but the music itself.

And now, on to the musicians.

But wait...an apology. A book of this nature is defined as much by what is left out as by what is included. Because I wanted to write detailed profiles of individuals, and not a broad, encyclopedic guide to women's music, I was forced to limit the number of people included. I had to neglect or accord only a few words to dozens of other Canadian women singer-songwriters whose work I admire and consider important: Nancy White, Edith Butler, Angèle Arsenault, k.d. Lang, Kate and Anna McGarrigle, Lillian Allen, Colleen Peterson, Arlene Mantle, Holly Arntzen, Shari Ulrich and many others. By not writing at length about their music I do not mean to slight them or to imply that their work has less excellence or validity than that of the women in this book.

To the seven musicians profiled here, I offer my admiration of their work and my sincere thanks for their interest and cooperation in this project.

And now—really—on to the musicians.

Connie Kaldor

The Canadian Croissant

"I write for people who don't have the ability to express themselves. Artists have the responsibility to speak for people."

Connie Kaldor strides across the stage flashing a radiant grin. She's wearing an extra-long turquoise suit jacket with rolled-up sleeves, tapered slacks, lacy white anklet socks and pointy-toed black shoes. Sitting down at the piano, she ruffles her hands through Norwegian-blond hair, pushes her sleeves up further, and taps out a few chords lightly, playfully, as if testing the water, knowing she's going to dive in anyway. "Imagine we're in Saskatchewan," she says, fingers tinkling the keys, "in a little town like Melford or Willow Bunch or Gravelburg. We're in the local truck stop cafe." One hand sweeps outward, palm down, while the other marks time on the piano. "You know, the kind with arborite countertops. The kind with pies under plastic covers in the little dessert case." The audience laughs and Kaldor smiles, still playing the same few chords. "The special is printed on a slip of paper and taped to the mirror. There's no fish on the menu, unless it comes in sticks." Another burst of laughter.

Kaldor points. "Over there, in the corner, is the jukebox. It's got everything: Twisted Sister, Patsy Kline, George Jones, the theme from 'Music Box Dancer,' Hank Williams, polkas. There are copies of the polka record for sale at the cash register." Her fingers play over the keys for a few moments. "And there's the waitress. It's ten o'clock in the morning and she's filling coffee cups for farmers who are discussing machinery and everybody's illnesses. She hasn't received too many tips lately — it's not a big deal in Saskatchewan to leave extra money lying around." The audience howls. "Now the *waitress is at the window,"* Kaldor continues. *"She clears a little space in the steam and watches the Greyhound bus pull out of the parking lot, bound for Regina."* The rhythm of the piano chords slides into a slow three-quarter tempo. *"She watches the bus go, and she wants to go with it."* Kaldor begins to sing in a quiet, low-pitched voice.

> *If you buy her a dream, she'll follow you anywhere*
> *To any old truck stop that this world might bring.*
>
> *Bird on a wing, bird on a wing*
> *She knows in her heart she was destined to fly*
> *Like a bird on a wing, bird on a wing*
> *She's waiting for you to fly by.*

She throws her head back, and her voice pours out of her arched throat like honey or sunshine as she reveals the secrets in the waitress's heart.

*A*ttending a Connie Kaldor concert is like going to the circus — a little of everything going on at once. There are anecdotes and jokes, love and longing and loneliness, all with a feminist backbone. There are snippets of Canadiana, folk-style ballads, rock and roll, country tunes, and music hall ditties, all done up in a voice that whispers, whoops, groans and purrs. And tying everything together is that mischievous smile, the child bursting out of the adult. Kaldor pulls it off because she excels in every aspect of musicianship: instrumental ability, voice, songwriting and performing. Many in the Canadian music industry call her the most complete woman singer-songwriter working today.

Connie Kaldor is a natural performer, one of those rare people who sparkle under the spotlight. One moment she is a comedienne, introducing herself as "the Canadian croissant," interspersing songs with humourous anecdotes, poking as much fun at herself as at other targets. The next moment she is a soulful songstress, delivering her songs with eyes closed, leaning into the piano as into an embrace or a windstorm. Jon Herman said in the *Boston Phoenix*, "...passionately clutching the microphone with one hand and casually tucking the cord behind her hip with the other, she's...adept at suggesting a brazen Broadway torch singer."

Given Kaldor's skill as a performer, it isn't surprising that she nearly became an actress. Born in Regina in 1953, she was a self-confessed "ham" at an early age. "I was always organizing shows. My friends and I put on fairs in my backyard. Gypsy tent, house of horrors, the whole thing. We charged one penny admission."

22

She performed in every talent show and play that high school offered and took acting classes at the Globe Theatre in Regina. After receiving a B.F.A. in theatre in 1975 from the University of Alberta, she pursued an acting career in Edmonton, Saskatoon and Toronto, establishing a reputation as a versatile and talented actress. She cites director Paul Thompson of Theatre Passe Muraille as an important mentor. Her favourite film role was as a mental patient in *Ada*, directed by Claude Jutra. "What a unique opportunity to work with such a wonderful director! I consider it a great honour."

But there were musical influences operating as well. Both of Connie's parents played the piano, and her father directed a church choir. Along with her brothers and sisters, she was forced to take piano lessons from the age of five. "I hated it, but I stuck it out— partly because my parents made me, and partly because my reward for passing grade eight piano was getting a guitar." That's when she started writing songs. "Practicing chord changes, I'd come up with lyrics. It made practicing less boring." This was the '60s, the era of folk music, and she modeled herself on solo acoustic folksingers like Joni Mitchell, Sylvia Tyson and Joan Baez. As well, Connie's older brother introduced her to groups like the Brothers Four and the Kingston Trio.

In 1970, while still in high school, she auditioned for the Regina Folk Festival. "I had written a song called 'Eaton's Inflatable Bra.' I think that got me my berth in the festival." With a repertoire of traditional and contemporary folk songs and a few original tunes, she sang at several workshops and was the opening act for one of the night-time main stage concerts. Because of her previous acting experience, she barely had stage fright ("just a bit of jitters"), even in front of the huge festival crowd. "What was the most fun was hanging out with real live musicians."

During university Kaldor gave guitar lessons and played the occasional gig to earn pocket money. Even after graduation, while working in theatre, she continued to write and play music on the side. But by the late '70s, she acknowledged she couldn't master both music and theatre. "I realized that I liked music better. I could write, and I wanted to be a creative person. As a singer-songwriter I figured I'd have more control over my life than I would as an actress."

In 1979 she embarked on her first concert tour, with Heather Bishop. They'd met a few years earlier when they were both singing at an N.D.P. fundraising picnic. "Heather was still with her band, Walpurgis Night," Connie says. "I was interested in feminism and thought an all-woman band was pretty neat. A friend of mine had urged me to contact them and maybe sing with them, but before I had a chance to, I met Heather at this picnic. I sang first. She liked

my stuff, befriended me and sat me down in front of a tape recorder —
she probably has some of the more embarrassing tapes of my career.''

Kaldor suggested that they do a joint tour of the prairies, with
each musician playing a solo set. Bishop agreed, and with a show
called "Saskatchewan Suite in Two Acts," they played Winnipeg,
Regina, Calgary, Edmonton and Saskatoon. "We booked any old
hall that we could get for nothing or next to nothing, and dragged
our friends along to do lights and sound. Believe it or not, we
actually made a little money." And they began a long personal and
professional friendship.

Afterwards Kaldor returned to Alberta to pursue a full-time
music career. She moved to Vancouver in 1984, then relocated to
Winnipeg in 1988. Although she loved the theatre, she has never
regretted her decision to be a musician. "I wouldn't change my life
now. Music gives me a lot of pleasure. I'm a better singer than I
would have been an actress."

In many ways she is a better singer *because* she was an actress.
She sees her show as a unified whole, not just a series of songs.
"In the theatre, the chance to be on stage is the most precious thing
in the world. That gives you a lot of discipline. I view my show as
really important, an opportunity to entertain people, not just to let
stuff out of my life." The theatre also gave her a sense of responsibility to her audience. She prepares seriously to perform. "That's
different from the music world where there's a mystique of showing
up in your old jeans and singing your songs, of trashing your hotel
room, of having contempt for your audience. I respect my audience."

And she is sensitive to the audience's response. "I constantly
monitor the impact of each song. If the audience doesn't respond
I ask myself, 'Did I set it up right? Is it formed right? Is the accompaniment to blame? Is it in the wrong place in the show?' You have to
be ruthless with your songs."

Kaldor wants to make her performances more theatrical. Her
eyes twinkling, she says, "I'd love to use stage sets. I want to do
more with the lighting — like in 'Get Back the Night' when we bring
the lights down to create an eerie atmosphere. I want to try having
the band members become characters in some of the songs, with
dialogue and action. For example, when I introduce one of my
polka tunes, I go into a rap about a prairie wedding in a small
church hall, where the jellied salad with miniature Kraft marsh-
mallows is on the buffet table and everybody's drinking rye and
Coke. Then I talk about how the drummer in the band, who happens
to be the bride's younger brother, just got a new set of drums from
the Sears catalogue for Christmas. Kris, our drummer, takes on the
persona of the novice drummer and starts playing this basic rhythm:
boom chicka boom chicka boom. No matter what the song, he

plays the same rhythm. We create the ambience of a small prairie town and it's really effective in setting the mood for the song. That's the kind of thing I want to do more of."

Kaldor hastens to add that she doesn't condone slapping special effects onto a show just to add sparkle. "First, the material has to be good. Then you can work in some dramatic touches to enhance it. We're a very visual society nowadays. People need visual stimulation, especially in a large hall. Theatrical elements can create an atmosphere, intensify the experience, help the audience focus in on the song."

And the more she puts into her show, the more she gets back. Performing is the payoff, the jolt of energy that brings the communication process full circle. "I love performing. People give back the energy. They're grateful that I've entertained them or made them think about something or touched their emotions. I can feel it in the dark when my audience is with me." Valdine Ciwko, Vancouver Folk Fest publicist says, "Connie has incredible control over her audience. She can hold them in her hand and do what she wants." Her band says simply, "She takes no prisoners."

Kaldor has taken her interest in theatre one step further by making a video based on "Get Back the Night." With the help of some Edmonton friends who run a video production company, she wrote a script to develop the central concept of the song: Women will no longer tolerate violence and will take action to "get back the night." Connie acted in the video which was shot in Vancouver in 1987 with sponsorship by the National Film Board and released early in 1988. She wants to get it on Video Hits in Canada and MuchMusic and MTV in the States. It will also be available through the N.F.B.

The stage lights go down to a spooky dimness. Only Kaldor's blond hair and white blouse glow in the dark. She rises from the piano bench and brushes her fingers across a synthesizer keyboard, which is on top of the piano. A metallic tinkling ripples through the hall. She begins to play a steady rhythm on the low notes, thump-thump-thump-thump, thump-thump-thump-thump, like a wooden hammer tapping a tin can. With her other hand she presses a high note that sounds like a distant wailing, then runs her fingers down a minor scale, the notes spiraling downward into darkness. She turns to face the audience. Her face looks ashen in the gloom, lit by a strange smile. A high note suddenly screams a warning.

She speaks softly. "From up in the sky, Moon has been watching what's been going on down here on earth. She doesn't like what she sees." Thump-thump-thump-thump. "Too much fear, too much evil in the darkness." Again the scale slides downward. "Moon isn't going to stand for it anymore. She's going to strike back." Eerie sounds wail, suddenly close by. Half-singing, half-speaking, she begins in a menacing tone:

Fear doesn't start with the night's dark places
It comes from those of the twisted sight
Moon saw them lurking in her shadows
She got angry, she wants back her night.

Abruptly Kaldor starts pounding out chords. She sings in full voice, defiantly.

She's gonna get back, get back, get back the night.

The last word fades into a moan. The thump-thump-thump-thump returns. A metallic siren pierces the even rhythm.

Connie is an accomplished guitarist and pianist—remarkable considering she's never had formal guitar lessons and since childhood she's studied piano for only a year or two. She's self-taught on the synthesizer. She handles every style from country to boogie-woogie, cowboy music to rock and roll, folk to new wave, although she is perhaps most skilled at playing piano ballads. For recording and performing, she deliberately chooses backup musicians who are better instrumentalists than she is. "If you're around good people your skills improve. Excellent musicians lift up my standards."

Kaldor's best instrument is her voice. "The guts of Tina Turner, the honesty of Joan Baez, the atmosphere of Harmonium," says Diane Collins of *Music Express*. Jon Herman, *Boston Phoenix*, calls it "a burnished contralto, chic and sexy but never guttural." She's been taking voice lessons since 1985 and credits this vocal training with helping to build strength, correct bad habits and expand her range, which was already considerable. Impressive breath control enables her to belt out notes and to hold them for what seems an impossible duration. She says with a hint of impatience, "My voice is just maturing. I've got to push it to its limits now."

Some critics have said that Kaldor, Joni Mitchell and Anne Murray possess the purest voices among Canadian women singers. Connie's voice is not as mellow as Murray's: it has more cracks, more of the darkness that Mitchell's has, though not yet the maturity. Like Ferron, she speaks, grunts, groans and sighs. The heartfelt way she sings reminds one of Rita MacNeil. But Kaldor's delivery is not as raw as MacNeil's; her voice is perhaps too musical to lose its bell-like quality even in the most heart-wrenching song. While Rita brings tears to your eyes, Connie sends a chill up your spine.

Not only is Kaldor's singing powerful—so are her songs. Ideas, images and melodies constantly jostle in her mind, and she usually works on a few songs at a time. "Inspiration strikes anywhere. I've written songs in cars, planes and bus depots." She doesn't write with a specific audience in mind, except when writing for children. "I write for myself," she says. "I write for an idea." She composes on piano, guitar and, increasingly, synthesizer. "The synthesizer has affected what I can do musically, and that affects how I write. I can get so many different sounds out of it, and they make me think of different things." She usually doesn't set out to write in a particular musical style, but lets the content and words find the music—except when she feels she's been concentrating too much on one style. "If I've been writing lots of slow lyrical tunes I'll force myself to work on a country number. Or if I'm stuck on a song, I'll set myself the task of doing something completely different—say, a song for an imaginary 1930s revue—to spark myself, get the juices flowing." She grins. "Sometimes I get good material out of that."

Kaldor finds inspiration everywhere, from intimate feelings to global observations. In *Canadian Composer* she discussed this in typically contradictory fashion, first expressing wonder at the source of her songs ("Creating a song is like being given a gift; it just comes to me"), then insisting that hard work is at least as important ("Songwriting isn't a mystic thing. You have to have an idea first"). She has never been one to shrink from exposing her own feelings and experiences in her songs. "I don't disguise anything," she says with a laugh. "You can't be precious with yourself."

Some songs resonate with such honesty that you intuitively feel they are autobiographical. "God Made Mamas to Cry," for example, begins, *"God gave mamas too much heart/And children that try to tear it apart,"* then becomes a plea for forgiveness: *"I know it doesn't seem fair/That I can't stop you from caring/And I just can't see/Why you got children like me."*

"Sheep Creek" is written in the persona of a down-and-out young man in Calgary:

> *I'm going up to Sheep, gonna climb me a mountain*
> *Gonna dangle my feet in a pure mountain stream*
> *Gonna fill up my lungs with Rocky Mountain air*
> *I'll be there, if only in my dreams.*

His voice is so full of joyous longing that we suspect these are really Kaldor's yearnings.

She also observes people, imagines their feelings and invents their lives in songs. Kaldor talks about the waitress in "Bird on a Wing": "I was sitting in a little cafe, watching her. I could almost hear her thoughts. I could feel what she wanted. I wrote her song." Another song-portrait is "Roy," about a man who has fallen on hard times and who dreams of better days, when

> *... the cops don't know his name*
> *And fear's not a click on a telephone line*
> *And the nights don't need cocaine.*

The dilemmas of real people, rather than the underlying issues, inspire Kaldor to write. "I may get upset about an issue like mining. But when I see a miner with coal dust on his face, that's what moves me to write. When I heard about a woman who'd been badly beaten by her husband, I wrote 'One Hit Leads to Another,' about wife-battering. I myself haven't known that kind of abuse, but I've watched people and thought about it and imagined what it would be like. You don't have to experience something to feel empathy."

The issue of inventing other people's lives is one on which singer-songwriters disagree. Marie-Lynn Hammond and Rita MacNeil almost always write about their own feelings and experiences because they believe that is the proper domain of the creative artist, the only one possible to know thoroughly. As Hammond puts it, "I wouldn't presume to speak for another person."

Other songwriters, like Kaldor, Murray McLauchlan and Sylvia Tyson, feel that people's real or imaginary lives are worthy subjects for composition. Connie expresses this attitude when she says, "As a songwriter I write for people who don't have the ability to express themselves. Artists have the responsibility to speak for people."

One of the major themes in Kaldor's work is love, from the joy of romance to the bitterness of betrayal. In 1983 she sang in Calais, Maine, a town on the New Brunswick border, as part of a tour called the Great Canadian Folk Music Express. The town inspired a tender love song:

I remember that night near Calais, Maine
It had the kind of stars you could wish on...

One of these days I'm going to fly to the stars
And find out why they shine
I have a feeling that the reason they do
Is to light up that moonlight heart of mine.

A new song, "Love Letters," celebrates the early stages of romance. "I've always thought it's wonderful how stupid love makes you," she says when introducing the song in concert. Then she sings about receiving mushy love letters:

I like the parts that make me blush
Oh, you devil, you
...I like the parts that you write in French
And I'm not quite sure what you say.

She also writes about the darker side of love. "Danger Danger" explores the temptation of infidelity: *"You've got one at home and you don't need this/But like a moth to a flame it's a lip to a kiss."*

The spurned lover in "I Go Out Walkin'" walks *"through the middle of midnight with a burning inside,"* as the synthesizer melody rolls over and over like raindrops or footsteps. Her lover's lies have pushed her beyond despair: *"There's nothing they can throw me that I can't throw back/Or at least know where to hide."* In the end she finds release: *"I cried on the shoulder of the road till I felt all right."*

Kaldor also writes about Canada. She is not alone: many contemporary singer-songwriters have explored Canadian themes in their music. Marie-Lynn Hammond, Stan Rogers, Gordon Lightfoot, Nancy White, Murray McLaughlan, Bob Bossin, Kate and Anna McGarrigle — this is only a partial list. But Connie Kaldor stands out for her frequent references to Canadian subjects. "Americans seem to have more pride in where they're from. Canadians are still reticent about being Canadian. We don't see our history or ourselves as being important — we've been told for so long by the British that our own feelings and interpretations are less important or less valid. And we've had a huge, powerful and very different culture right next door. So we've tended not to express our own visions in the arts. When I was starting out, it was unusual for a singer to sing about Canada."

Despite this, or perhaps because of it, Kaldor has made her identity as a Canadian an important part of her work. She proudly claims her prairie roots. "The prairies are dear to my heart. They've shaped who I am. I want to mythologize my home." Yet in the next breath she insists, "I don't see myself as a prairie songwriter. I see myself as international." Disclaimers aside, she has written many songs about Canadian history, land, climate and culture, and doesn't hesitate to present them to American audiences, providing historical or cultural background when necessary. "By the time I've finished explaining 'Batoche,' Americans probably know more about the Riel Rebellion than most Canadians," she jokes.

> *On the South Saskatchewan River*
> *There's a crossing and bend that they call Batoche*
> *And on the banks of that river*
> *A battle was won and a people were lost.*

Still, she feels a special resonance when she sings to Canadian audiences, a sense of identification and pride.

One Canadian subject that she tackles is the French-English issue. "Au Revoir Bye Bye" humourously examines the difficulties of carrying on a cross-cultural love affair, and, on a deeper level, the ignorance and mistrust that divide the two groups.

> *Ta mère and ton père te disent que ce n'est pas très bien*
> *Ils connaient que je viens de l'ouest*
> *Ce n'est pas the best, eh?*
>
> *(Your mother and father tell you that this isn't proper*
> *They know I come from the west*
> *That's not the best, eh?)*

But she sees no way out of their predicament:

Je te donne mon coeur, my love
And I swear by the bon dieu above
That I love you, je t'aime
But I'm English—I am.

Canadian landscape also features prominently in Connie Kaldor's work. "Wood River," a love song, is set beside a small Saskatchewan river. "It's a user-friendly river," she says when introducing the song in concert, "not like the Fraser, which—" dramatic piano chords "—is a serious river." Gentle tinkling on the piano. "No, the Wood River is just a lazy trickle, meandering along without going anywhere. And that's just fine with all the lovers in the Gravelburg region, who like to park along its willowy banks."

Kaldor's Canadian heritage shows up musically as well as thematically. The prairies gave her a country influence, found in songs like "Sheep Creek," with its twangy steel guitar. "Margaret's Waltz" is based on an old fiddle tune, and Connie has in her repertoire a few Ukrainian-style polkas. A new song, "Outlaw," is a feminist cowboy song with a rolling guitar line that sounds like horses' hoofbeats. Connie loves country music but jokes, "I'm not right-wing enough to be a country singer," adding more seriously, "I don't want to cut myself off from other kinds of music that I care about."

Whatever their style, all of Kaldor's songs grow from a strong sense of feminism. She defines feminists as "people who actively work to change the status of women in society," and she doesn't count herself as one of these. Yet she has always, by her own example, worked for self-determination and equality for women. "I'm an artist who has a stance because I'm a woman singing about women's concerns. In that sense I'm a feminist. My feminism is a by-product of the way I live. When I was starting out it was a big deal that I was a solo woman singer writing my own songs and running my own career. I was expected to stand for every women's issue. It's different now. There are more women doing it. That's a sign of health."

Connie cites Sylvia Tyson, Joni Mitchell, Catherine McKinnon, Carole King, Kate and Anna McGarrigle and Marie-Lynn Hammond as women singer-songwriters who served as role models for her. Now she sees herself as a model for younger women musicians like Lucie Blue Tremblay. "Ferron, Heather Bishop and I have changed attitudes towards women musicians in this country. We've opened doors, just by being successful."

Her feminism shows up in varied and unexpected ways. "One Hit Leads to Another" and "Get Back the Night" are serious political statements. "Jerks" takes the subject of sexual harrassment and wraps it in a comical package. Gary Cristall, director of the Vancouver Folk Music Festival, recalls, "The first time Connie played that song at the festival there were screams of delight from women in the audience because it related to their experience. They'd always been waiting for someone to write that song."

Kaldor's fingers slide up the piano keyboard, playing a few chords along the way. She begins to tap out a lively, staccato rhythm. "This song is about certain streets where it's dangerous to walk. Not because of rapists or muggers or skateboarders. No, because of — " She leans close to the microphone and whispers confidentially, " — jerks." The audience laughs. She continues to tap out the back-beat. "Yes, this is for all of you females who need to be reminded about the features of your anatomy to know that you're really a — " She lifts one eyebrow and slurs in a deep, sexy voice, " — woman." Laughter and whoops from the audience. Grinning, Connie plays the refrain, a little louder now. "You're walking down the street, on your way to a power lunch or to return your library books, when you hear an all-too-familiar sound." She gives a piercing wolf whistle. "Right away you know it's the — "

Jerks! With a capital J. Hey, hey, hey, hey, baby.

They're always in packs or groups of two

And like sharks in a pool they descend on you

... They're standing at the corner just to watch you walk

Don't meet their eye or they'll plague you for blocks.

By the third chorus the audience is joining her in shouting out "Jerks!" When the song is over, there are cheers, laughter and a few lewd whistles.

The women's audience has been an important support in Kaldor's career. On a practical level, women have come to her concerts, bought her records, and lobbied to have her included on folk festival rosters. Her audience has also been a fount of inspiration for her songs. She believes that music can be a powerful social catalyst, affecting not only women's rights but all issues. "People are a force for change, and music moves people," she said in *Canadian Composer*. Lois Path, writing in *Images*, quoted her as saying, "You need to sneak up on people with politics.... When you touch people, then you've changed them." Kaldor adds, "Music is a rallying cry. Dolly Parton singing 'Nine to Five' has done more to change attitudes than hundreds of speeches."

Things *are* changing, she says, citing the existence of more women songwriters and backup musicians than before, more women in unconventional genres like punk and jazz. But women still must work harder and be better than men to get jobs, she says, and they remain under-represented in record production, broadcasting and management. Still, she is optimistic: "The fact that women are writing will change what's out there. I'm glad to be a woman living in this time."

For Kaldor, the flip side of feminism is the strength that we all must find within ourselves. Rather than waiting for someone—probably a man—to transform her life, the truck stop waitress realizes that she can *"be her own bird on a wing."* In "Strength, Love and Laughter," feminism and inner resolve are intertwined: *"Woman, you're gonna need some strength just to get through / Woman, you've got to find that strength deep inside of you / ...Deep like a river, you've got to dig down deep."*

The idea of inner strength, in turn, is connected to the notion of taking chances. To a hard-driving rock beat, "Wanderlust" celebrates *"the little bit of gypsy in everyone's heart."* Her sense of humour comes through in the whining voice of caution:

> *You can't quit your job, you can't leave school*
> *If you just take it easy you can work your way up in the typing pool.*

But she urges us to ignore that prudent advice: *"Don't just take it easy—take a good map and go."* Underneath the fun is a message: taking chances is necessary for the health of the soul. And Kaldor doesn't just write about risk-taking—she practices it, both musically and in the management of her career.

Does she ever wish for a calmer, more secure life? "For about five minutes," she deadpans. "I like being a renegade. I like playing the part of the fool, testing the limits of what people can take, putting them a little off-guard. It helps open them up and keeps me interested. One good thing about the music industry is that it's always changing—it keeps you from getting stale. But this way of living is tiring and hectic, and you run the risk of getting exhausted and giving less effort. If you practice being mediocre, you'll get good at it." She laughs, but she means it. She is aware of the temptation of coasting on her considerable vocal and musical talent and not pushing herself to achieve greater artistry. Yet her fiercely creative spirit won't let her settle for mediocrity. So she keeps trying new things—musical styles, performance techniques, subjects for songs, instruments—always daring to learn and to change.

One experiment is her collaboration with Roy Forbes, a British Columbia singer-songwriter also known as Bim. Their partnership came about at the suggestion of Claire Lawrence, a Vancouver-based musician, arranger and producer, who had worked with both of them. "The first time we met, Roy brought some music he had written. He had the phrase 'It must be love or something,' but no other words. We jammed and worked out the lyrics. We hit it off right away."

Forbes is a country-rock singer in the Hank Williams-Elvis Presley tradition, and his blues sensibility is a perfect counterpoint to Kaldor's lyricism. In "Love or Something," the tune that came out of that first meeting, they use a Marvin Gaye-Tammy Terrell-type vocal alternation in a bluesy rock and roll arrangement. She wonders about the strange new sensation she's feeling: *"Is it the wine? Could it be the flu?/All I know is that I'm blaming you,"* while he confesses: *"I'm not good at memorizing/Well, I know every crease in your jeans."* Reg Silvester, in the *Edmonton Journal*, says, "The combination of those two voices—Bim's rich, throaty falsetto and Kaldor's range from honeyed alto to smooth soprano—is pure joy."

Just as the chemistry of attraction described in the song is a mystery, so, for Connie, is the success of her collaboration with Roy. "There's no explaining how it works, it just does. It's rare to find someone like that with whom you have a creative connection." But one factor of which she is certain is Forbes's musicianship. "He's brilliant, one of the musicians I respect most in this country. He's got vast musical knowledge, a great ear and very high standards. When you work with somebody that good, you just click." She says that they communicate well despite different approaches to song-writing. "He's much more organized than I am. I'm more devil-may-care in my writing. He's got all his songs written down properly in notebooks. Mine are half-written on scraps of paper." The two musicians test ideas on each other and stretch one another creatively and musically. "We needle each other to work," Kaldor says with a grin. "Roy calls and says, 'Hi, got anything new?' and I think, 'Oh, God, I'd better get busy.'"

Kaldor and Forbes have toured together, performing solo and as a duet. Besides "Love or Something," they have co-written several children's songs. In 1986 they made an album of original and traditional Christmas songs, *New Songs for an Old Celebration*, on Festival Records. The album received considerable CBC Radio play and led to several concerts, including a series with the Vancouver Symphony Orchestra.

Many of Kaldor's fans are unaware that she's written dozens of children's songs—though given her zany personality, they probably wouldn't be surprised. One kids' tune is an ode to that much-ignored feature of anatomy, the bellybutton: *"When things are really bad and looking pretty grim/I simply lift up my shirt and stick my finger in."* In "Hippopotamus" we learn:

> *If you love a hippopotamus and you love her alotamus*
> *She will be your friend*
> *Than can be mighty handy now and then.*

In a mock-operetta, "Slug Song," she celebrates the maligned creatures, who plead: *"It's not our fault if we're slimy and brown."*

Kaldor has performed at the Vancouver Children's Festival (in 1985 with Heather Bishop and in 1986 with Roy Forbes) and on children's stages at various folk festivals. Bishop has recorded several Kaldor tunes on her own children's albums, with Connie singing backup, and Kaldor has recently made an album of children's lullabies in English and French with Carmen Campagne (formerly with Folle Avoine).

While she enjoys performing for children, she doesn't want to make a career of it. "It requires so much energy, and the material is limiting," she says. "Yet at the same time it's limitless. I can write songs about slugs or hippos or whatever I like. Performing for kids brings out the brat in me... and I love being a brat."

Despite the enjoyment she gets from writing and performing, Kaldor is often frustrated by the progression of her career. She feels her reputation isn't as extensive as her talent warrants. She wants to expand her audience beyond the feminist, folk and Canadian components, but isn't sure how. This dilemma has accompanied her career like a shadow.

Connie raised the money and independently produced her first album, *One Of These Days*, in 1981. It's best classified as folk, though it's a mix of styles, including country, rock, folk and gospel. The production is low-key, focusing on her expressive voice and piano-playing, with judicious use of backup instrumentals and vocals. The album received favourable reviews, limited radio play, and modest sales.

Artistically Kaldor was pleased with *One Of These Days*; commercially she was not. On the verge of her second album she decided to take some stylistic chances and put out a more commercial product. "I wanted to get airplay. I wanted to break out of the folk slot and reach a wider audience." On a Maritimes tour in 1983 she met Claire Lawrence and was impressed by his technological expertise and knowledge of the commercial market. He produced her second album, *Moonlight Grocery*, which cost $60,000 and took six months to record. Released on Kaldor's independent Coyote Records label, it was later picked up for distribution by Redwood Records in the U.S. By early 1988 it had sold about 20,000 copies.

Connie found working with Claire instructive. "He's an experienced producer, a real professional, who sets a high standard in the studio. He forced me to examine what I wanted to do with every song, rather than just doing things out of habit. For example, I originally wrote 'Get Back the Night' in the traditional folksong way—verse, chorus, verse, chorus. It had eight verses. Claire got me to restructure and tighten it up, and it worked much better. He also taught me how to take control in the recording studio, how to listen, to ask for and demand certain sounds, to speak out when I didn't like what I was hearing. I learned that what I expect, I can get.''

Lawrence fulfilled Kaldor's wish for a more commercial record. The backup band is larger and more instrumentally varied than on *One Of These Days*. The sound is much more technologically sophisticated, in places almost new wave. Several songs have aggressive, driving rhythms and synthesizer accompaniment. But not all of *Moonlight Grocery* is in the pop-rock vein. "Calais, Maine," "Talk Without Speaking," "Wood River" and "Bird on a Wing" are in the simpler style of her first album, with greater emphasis on vocals and piano.

The result is a collection ranging from electronic rock to acoustic folk — in short, a typically Kaldorean mixed bag. Critical reaction, like the album, has been mixed. In the *Province* Tom Harrison wrote, "*Moonlight Grocery* is a thoroughly realized album that manages to contain the many facets of her personality....(It) establishes Kaldor as a superb songwriter." The *Globe and Mail* applauded her willingness to dive into emotional pools: "...not just a dip of the toes, mind you, but a bare-naked midnight dive right in over her head, and that takes courage."

Other reviews have faulted the album for containing too many different moods and styles, and for being over-produced. In *Mariposa Notes*, Diana Tyndale said, "Her voice sounds strained and lacking in depth, overpowered by complex instrumentals, heavy percussion and electronic effects." Diane Collins of *Music Express* wrote, "The production is flat, cold, clinical and entirely unsuited to a woman who radiates this much passion."

Kaldor shrugs. "Part of making a record is taking chances, working with people who pull you in new directions. I knew there would be a hue and cry over this album, especially from people who knew me as a folksinger and expected me to sound the same. But I wanted to try new things. If you can't do that, you might as well give up. I might as well do 'Tie a Yellow Ribbon 'Round the Old Oak Tree' — I'd make more money at it."

She agrees that her voice is sometimes overpowered by the electronic effects, but says, "I wanted radio play, and I got it, to some extent. When you make an album there's always things you want to change afterwards. When you're in the studio you like the sound, but time teaches you what works and what doesn't. *Moonlight Grocery* may not be *the* Connie Kaldor album; maybe that'll come in a couple of them. But it's definitely professionally done with great musicians and a lot of risks taken. Pulling together many styles has always been a problem with my stuff — not for me but for radio programmers who want to slot it as pop, rock, folk, country, whatever. I still get put in the folk bin, though that's not my image anymore." She gives an exasperated smile. "I don't know what my image is. I just do what I do."

Many singer-songwriters struggle to find a balance between singing from the heart and achieving popular success. Some, like Bruce Springsteen, Paul Simon, Rita MacNeil and Bruck Cockburn, appear to have discovered the right combination. Others, like Shari Ulrich and Connie Kaldor, have not — yet. Neither content solely with the folk music market, nor willing to manufacture mindless pop tunes, Kaldor is still searching for her commercial niche. She ranks with the best Canadian and American woman singer-songwriters, but is still relatively unknown in the North American music scene. She now has enough good new songs for another album. But she hasn't yet picked a producer or chosen backup musicians and won't proceed until she has a good distribution deal in place. "I don't know what the sound of the next album will be, pop or whatever, but I want it to sound like me. I want the vocals to be key. I want it to have heart.

"It would be nice to make it in the business, but it's not worth turning myself into a commercial package. You've got to write from your heart. You've got to be happy. You've got to be saying something. It's not enough for me to just have money in the bank." She grins, putting up her hand. "Don't get me wrong, I'd love to have lots of money in the bank. But I want to make it doing things I love. That's why I've stayed an independent for so long: it's good for my mental health. Success is a relative thing. Somehow looking at my bank balance has never given me the hit that singing has."

Connie Kaldor runs her fingers aimlessly over the piano keys, hitting notes here and there, then settles over a few chords, which she plays lightly in a repeating sequence. "This song is about being good. Capital G Good. You've been trying to be a Good Boy or a Good Girl. You've been following all your New Year's resolutions to a T." A ripple of laughter. "You've been listening to public affairs broadcasts on the CBC." More laughter. Still playing the same chords, she whines, "You haven't been eating any sugar; you've been listening to the hog reports at noon." The rhythm of the chords gets faster, their volume louder. "You've had your hand on the pulse of the nation — and you've had it with the pulse of the nation." The audience roars. Kaldor grins. "What you really want is the pulse of a stranger, and the closer the better." The chords turn into a boogie-woogie beat, a la Jerry Lee Lewis. As Connie pounds it out, she taps her feet and her hair shakes in rhythm. "Yes, what you need is a trip down to the — "

Moonlight grocery, moon, moonlight grocery...
I want to sip on a dusty bottle that comes with a mouldy cork
I want to buy something illegal, grab someone I'll regret
Roar around downtown in my brother's red Corvette.

Her fingers strike the last chord and stay poised, arched over the keys. Her head is thrown back, so that her body, from her foot reaching forward to the piano pedal, to the hair trailing behind her, forms a rough diagonal line. Her eyes are closed. In the moment of silence before the applause begins, a smile spreads across her face.

By My Life Be I Spirit

"I have a feeling inside of me that does not have words. I go deep, deep into that feeling. It creates a couple of chords. They're lonely and they crack something and the music and words come together."

Ferron walks across the darkened stage and steps into the circle of light at the centre. She wears a black tuxedo-like suit, white shirt and thin black tie. Within moments everyone in the audience is clapping. She pulls her guitar strap over her shoulder, her face expressing a mixture of fear, amusement and gratitude, as if she can't quite believe that this reception is really for her. "I wish I just had to tap dance for you," she says with a wry grimace, "but I have to play the guitar and sing." The audience laughs. Ferron smiles — a tentative smile, not daring to become a grin. Yet.

She begins to finger-pick a rolling refrain in three-quarter time. "I'm big on self-pity," she says dryly. The audience laughs. "I remember all of my most satisfying pouts." Louder laughter. A smile flickers across her face. "That's a dead end, eh?" Chuckles of appreciation. "You can only go so far with self-pity. After a while it gets boring. But if you admit you're bored, you have to do something about it — like find something to be happy about." She pauses. "And you don't want to do that." Laughter and scattered applause from the audience.

The guitar refrain gets louder. Ferron sways slightly from side to side.

> *I thank you your letters though they come to me slowly*
> *I hear the city's in a panic with its first foot of snow*

*Her voice is gritty, as if she'd swallowed sand. On the high notes
it cracks. It sounds parched.*

> *And it's everyone's secret and muttered refrain*
> *That for all of our trouble we be lonely again*
> *It's old human nature, it's cold or it's hot*
> *But if it's snowin' in Brooklyn*
> *I'd say snow's what we've got.*

*L*ogically, Ferron should not be a star. She doesn't have a pretty voice. She's not an excellent guitarist. She's low-key and understated, even on stage. She rarely gives interviews and has dropped out of the music scene for as long as a year at a time, to rest, recharge and write.

Yet she *is* a star, at least within the sphere of folk and women's music. Her last two albums together have sold more than 80,000 copies. The magic words "Ferron concert" produce instantly sold-out houses—some as large as 2,000-seat halls. Despite her sporadic schedule, her fans remain unshakably loyal.

Why? Her songs. They're poetic gems, reflecting meaning from numerous facets. And, like the most luminous stones, they pull us into their glow, deep into our own vision, so that we too discover the source of their light.

Lots of songwriters can put together a phrase, capture a feeling, create an image. But Ferron goes beyond this. She lives in and writes from a place of intense emotion and deep spirituality, pursuing a genuine search for selfhood that takes her so far inside that it ultimately links her to the universe. Gayle Scott, her manager for the last eight years, said in a 1984 radio interview in Berkeley, California, "There are channels open in her that aren't open in most others. Most people spend lifetimes trying to get access to them. Ferron just sort of wakes up there."

Even her name springs from an subconscious source. Roughly translated from the French, it means a mixture of iron and rust. Years ago a housemate of hers dreamed that Ferron received the name. She adopted it and has used no other ever since.

Talking to Ferron is like taking a seminar in philosophy, music, ethics and creativity. Instead of discussing album sales and musical technique, she talks about the creative process, dreams and the mystery of songwriting. She often refers to "the path." "I feel that I'm a spirit who became a person," she says. "All of my desire on earth is to become a human being. My sense of spirit has always been more consistent than my sense of people. Maybe we're all

spirit condensed into personhood through the womb. We lose our spiritual memory because we can't use it here on earth. But later we will expand into spirit again."

Balancing her metaphysical preoccupations is a strong physical presence — short, compactly built, with a low centre of gravity, close to the earth. Under short, bluntly-cut, reddish-brown hair, her face is a collection of strong features: prominent, straight nose, high cheekbones, squarish jaw. "Ferron's face mirrors Canadian history — half Anglican assurance, half immigrant sweat," said a *Boston Phoenix* reviewer.

In conversation Ferron looks right into your eyes and chooses her words with care. She laughs a lot, a deep, chesty laugh, then becomes moist-eyed at moving memories. She gestures with her hands, underlining what she is saying. She lives in this world with the rest of us — but not all of her, all the time. Part of the time she is gazing upon a vast inner realm, and the vision she sees there guides her writing and her life. In *Valley Women's Voice*, Kathleen Moran said, "(She is a) lens through which we other beings can sense the mystical movements of the universe."

Perhaps the most spiritual and best-loved of Ferron's songs is "Testimony," the title track of her third album. The song has become something of a feminist anthem, the quintessential statement of all that women's music seeks to express. Yet she wrote it at a time when she felt weak, vulnerable and confused. She had been asked to write a song for a National Film Board movie called *This Film is About Rape*. Since she had suffered sexual abuse herself, she decided to use her experience as a starting point for the song. She went to the police station to look up the record of her assault, but couldn't get any information. Frustrated and blocked, she began to worry that she wouldn't finish the song in time.

In the midst of this anxiety, Ferron attended the Michigan Women's Music Festival for the first time. Under a full moon, she heard the *a capella* gospel group Sweet Honey in the Rock. "I had never felt such power," she says. "I started to cry — with love, with jealousy. I wanted to do that work." Returning home, she wrote "Testimony." "I was terrified to sing it and have people realize my weakness. I was bewildered when it became an anthem of strength." Years later she sang the song with Sweet Honey, and both she and they separately recorded it. In Ferron's version, the violin sings a sweet refrain, carrying the melody round and round.

> *Listen — there are waters hidden from us*
> *In the maze we find them still*
> *We'll take you to them, you take your young ones*
> *May they take their own in turn*

And by our lives be we spirit
And by our hearts be we women
And by our eyes be we open
And by our hands be we whole.

That expression of spiritual unity is not what you'd expect from someone of Ferron's background. The oldest of seven children, she was born in Ontario in 1952 to a French Canadian mother and an English Canadian father. The family moved to British Columbia when she was five, and she was raised in Richmond, a suburb of Vancouver. Her first language was French, but she learned English as a young child. Remarking that people notice unusual pronunciation and phrasing in her speech, she says, "I think switching languages while I was young affected the way I learned to speak." Gradually she forgot almost all her French, except in dim memories.

Ferron's mother played the guitar, and when French Canadian relatives visited, the family gathered their guitars, banjos, violins and washboards, and sang country music and traditional French Canadian songs. But musical sharing was the exception rather than the rule. Most of the time Ferron felt isolated within her family. "I grew up in silence. Nobody talked. It drove me crazy." As well, she was a stranger to the popular culture around her, unfamiliar with folk and rock music of the times. She didn't hear Bob Dylan or the Beatles until she was in her twenties. "I kept confusing Dylan and Dion," she says with perfect seriousness.

She learned to play guitar at age eleven. Her mother taught her some chords, and she learned others from a book, but never took formal lessons. "To this day I don't feel I'm an accomplished guitarist. I use it as a vehicle to express what I want to say." As soon as she could play a few chords, she began to write songs. "My family didn't understand. They said, What's wrong with 'May the Circle Be Unbroken?' So I retreated into the songwriting, and the music became *mine*." A year later she had written one hundred songs — and discovered how to break the silence in which she was trapped. "Music was a way to talk, a medium for communicating. I found a way to live by playing the guitar. Music became my life source."

Although Ferron's music was mostly private, she did hear some contemporary music and was strongly influenced by certain singer-songwriters. One of these was Joni Mitchell. "There isn't a woman singer today who hasn't been affected by Joni as both a singer and a woman." Ferron was fourteen when she heard both Judy Collin's and Joni Mitchell's versions of "Both Sides Now" on the radio. "I liked Joni Mitchell's version and not Judy Collins's, but I didn't know why. I didn't know that people recorded other people's songs.

But I could hear the difference. That was my first inkling of delivery."

Another important influence was Leonard Cohen. The first time she heard one of his songs — "Hey That's No Way to Say Goodbye" — she was impressed by tne complexity of his thoughts and the craftsmanship of his writing. Later, when she compared his rough delivery of his own songs to the melodious version sung by Jennifer Warnes, she reacted as she had with Collins and Mitchell. "Warnes sings the songs, but he delivers up a part of himself. That's what I always want to do. Cohen was always on a path, and still is; he works from a path." Other musical influences were Janis Ian, Hank Williams, Neil Young, Bruce Cockburn and Gordon Lightfoot.

Ferron left home at sixteen to work in factories, shovel gravel, waitress and drive taxi, while continuing to write songs and play them for herself and close friends. "At parties my contribution was to offer songs in an insecure voice." Her friends urged her to sing publicly, but she was too scared. Finally, in 1975, she agreed to play at a benefit for Press Gang publishers in Vancouver. At her debut performance, before five hundred people, she found an audience that loved her music. Over the next few years, she sang at other benefits, women's events and small coffee houses in Vancouver, mostly to audiences of women, and built a small but dedicated following.

By 1977 Ferron had a large repertoire of original songs. Her friends encouraged her to make an album. They contributed their own money and raised the rest, and that year she released *Ferron* on her own Lucy Records label. "It was recorded in a video studio on two-track equipment. The production quality was pretty poor. It was just me and a guitar." Nevertheless all one thousand copies sold quickly. The following year she released *Ferron Backed Up,* recorded under the same circumstances, except this time she played with a small band. The second album sold out as quickly as the first; both are now collector's items.

By then Ferron had graduated from tiny coffee houses to the Soft Rock Cafe in Vancouver's Kitsilano district, playing five-night stints to full houses. But she was still timid, uncommunicative, afraid of the audience, afraid to expose her intimate music to them, yet needing to. "I couldn't look at the audience or talk between songs. I would just sort of sit there and mumble away at my songs and wonder what the hell I was doing there." She had a fistful of brilliant songs but no idea how to build a career, or even an inkling that it was possible.

Then she met Gayle Scott, a photographer and film-maker from Los Angeles. Gail became her manager, producer, business partner and, as Ferron says, "guardian angel." Gayle took control of Ferron's career, shaping her image, attending to business details, booking gigs and, most important, helping her gain confidence as a performer. "Gayle told me I could try to talk between songs," Ferron recalls. "She helped me realize that the audience wasn't coming to hurt me or because they hated me. They were coming because they loved me and wanted to hear what I had to offer. Very slowly I learned to relax and open up onstage."

In 1980 Ferron and Gayle borrowed $27,000 and recorded the album *Testimony*, this time in a proper studio with excellent musicians. Distributing it themselves, they sold five thousand copies in four months. Two years later the record was released in the United States on the Philo label, and still sells steadily. Critics raved about *Testimony*. In the *New York Times*, Stephen Holden called it "reminiscent in its sylvan textures of *Astral Weeks*, Van Morrison's moody rock masterpiece."

In 1984 Ferron released *Shadows on a Dime*, co-produced by Gayle and jazz-rock singer Terry Garthwaite. This was her breakthrough album. Publications across North America were full of praise. Don Shewey of *Rolling Stone* gave it a four-star rating: "a feast of excellent musicianship and fine songwriting...cowgirl meets Yeats." Redwood Records released the album in the U.S., and Ferron recently signed a deal with Musik Entente, a German company, for distribution throughout Europe.

Applause fades from the previous song, and Ferron's face grows serious. With a nod, she motions her band to begin. The drum pounds out a slow, heavy beat — angry, doomed. The electric guitars whine in a minor key. The viola bow rasps across the strings.

Ferron strums her guitar softly, with her usual gentle touch. But her body is tense, pulled in, coiled around the instrument. Is she protecting it, or is it protecting her?

She begins a song about a brutally painful childhood. At times she whispers, at times she sneers. Her voice rides the edge between despair and contempt.

I had to get out.

She sings of a mirror in which she sees her mother, her sister, her aunt — trapped.

I was afraid I'd see myself.

Each drum crash is like a blow to the body. The guitars play a tumble of descending notes. The viola wails like a siren.
Ferron lifts her head.

White winged mercy, don't you leave me here
White winged mercy, don't you leave me here.

45

> *She closes her eyes, clutching at salvation on mysterious white wings.*
> ©Ferron, Nemesis Publishing

Ferron weaves dreams, autobiography and observations into her songs. On the cover of *Shadows on a Dime*, she quotes Yeats: "The spirit is compelled to live over and over again the events that had most moved it...in the order of their intensity or luminosity.... (Then) the spirit must live through past events in the order of their occurrence....until all are related and understood, turned into knowledge."

Ferron relives past events by writing songs—an intuitive and often painful process of self-discovery. She has been quoted as saying, "If my public life ended tomorrow, I don't think I could stop writing. It's how I articulate my reality for myself. My thoughts are not linear, which makes for kind of a hard life. The writing is a good way to make it make sense, to make me make sense....I write when I feel very excited about something extremely private and internal and I don't know what it is....Sometimes I wish all I had to say was, 'Baby, baby, it's you.' But that's not what I want to say."

She can't explain where the inspiration comes from. "I have a feeling inside of me that does not have words. I go deep, deep into the feeling. It creates a couple of chords. They're lonely and they crack something and the music and words come together....The way I write is not orderly, it's fast and wild. Things move off other things. When I write, I'm allowed to trap all of that." Although the words and music emerge together, she recognizes their different natures: "Music is archetypal. Words are human spirit trying to bend reality."

Ferron compares writing a song to building a house without a blueprint. "You get it up bit by bit but you don't know how you did it. Someone says, 'Did you design that house?' You say, 'I built it but I didn't design it.' 'Can I see the plans?' 'There are no plans.' I go into a feeling and the feeling gives me a first line, which is like the foundation—it has to be right or the song falls apart. Then I add a wall over here and windows over there and a roof. I keep adding lines until it's built."

"Ain't Life a Brook" was built this way. "It was in the middle of winter. I was living in a place with no heat. I had cut some gloves so I could play the guitar. I was playing some chords in a funny rhythm that had been going around in my head. I felt something. What was it? I played it over and over, and began to see something: a person reading a book. I wrote that down and let it lead me in. There was a feeling of waiting. Those were waiting chords. What were they waiting for? I followed the feeling and found out that the person was waiting to leave. I played a G chord and the first chorus came to me."

Life don't clickety-clack down a straight line track
It comes together and it comes apart
You say you hope I'm not the kind to make you feel obliged
To go ticking through your time with a pained look in your eyes
You give me the furniture, we'll divide the photographs
Go out to dinner one more time, have ourselves a bottle of wine
and a couple of laughs.

©Ferron, Nemesis Publishing

"The song took fourteen hours to write. When it was finished, it had three choruses. Each chorus tells about some change that the person left behind is going to make. Partly the song is an expression of how I always felt incapable of coming through with friends in the way that people are supposed to do for each other. I don't think I was ever as high as the person in the song. I got a moment of clarity, of what you're supposed to be like. Just for a moment I understood."

"Shadows on a Dime" grew from the same kind of intuitive process. Ferron was on a train, on her way to sing at Folk City in New York. She felt terrified, honoured and incredulous all at once. As she sat looking out the window at the leaves going by in a blur, she went into a trance. "In a few minutes my life went by in five-year jumps. Fifteen years ago, working in the factory. Ten years ago, I got my guitar. Five years ago, Gayle came into my life. And now, this success.

"Just before I saw the buildings of New York the conductor came over and said, 'Excuse me, lady, can I have your ticket?' I gave him my ticket and then the buildings of New York came into view. But I didn't write anything down. I didn't know I was writing the song. I was just feeling all these things. I was living it. I went to New York, played the concert, and left. When I got to Ottawa, I took pencil and paper and, starting with the window frame of the train car, I wrote it all down. I had sat on the train facing backwards, and I wrote the song backwards, from the present to the factory. I realized that we all mark our future by where we've been. It made me assess where I'm going to be next.

"As I was writing, I remembered some chords I'd been practicing. I grabbed my guitar. The chords fit right in. I finished the song with music and then I cried and cried....Even now I don't fully understand 'Shadows.' When people ask, 'What do you mean by this or that?' I have to say, 'I don't know, I wish I could tell you.' But I love that song. It's God's gift to me."

"Shadows on a Dime" has a steady rhythm like a train rolling down the track, and a three-note guitar refrain goes up, up, up like a question asked over and over.

47

This window makes a perfect frame
For New England leaves like summer rain
They hold me as I hold this train
All shadows on a dime....

But I don't forget about the factory
I don't expect this ride to always be
Can I give you what you want to see?
Can we do it one more time?

Ten years have worn this guitar down
Its ivory whites are now mustard brown....
Where would I be without its ring?
Who would I be if I didn't sing?...

And now a tired conductor passes by
He takes my ticket with a sigh....
I imagine him with his hair jet black
Does he hide his fiddle in the back?
He gauged his words as the train went slack
The New York train stops here....

These windows make a perfect frame
For New York buildings like upright trains
They hold me as I hold the rain
Fleeting shadows on a dime.

Ferron says that the direction of her songwriting is from the personal to the universal, "from a person to a nation to a planet. 'Testimony' starts with me and ends up with me. 'Misty Mountain' starts with me alone in a dark room and ends with all of us in the corners, fighting, never closing our eyes. I resolve my fears by finally writing to a place where I am everyone."

She usually writes with pencil and paper. Recently she bought a computer, but felt uninspired sitting in front of the monitor. Then her dog chewed through the cable. "Once the computer was gone, and I was back to pencil and paper, I started writing again." She avoids trying to instruct or moralize in her songs. "If I get too pedantic or self-conscious, the songs hobble along for a while and just die." She generally writes in one sitting — sometimes a grueling one — and usually does not rewrite. "I might change a line or move a verse, but if I start rewriting I'm too much in the way."

Ferron's newer material moves in a slightly different direction from her earlier songs. "When I was young I had to write about isolation and separation. Now I'm trying to articulate optimism, to express my faith that there's shadow and light and that we have a choice." Although she has written some new songs along those lines, she is ruthless in judging her own work and will not release her next album until she has enough material that meets her own standards.

Meanwhile, she keeps writing. "I feel like I'm at the edge of the lake but I'm not *in* the lake. I'm just waiting for a sign. A lot of it is magic." While waiting for that sign, she tries to make herself ready: "My writing will come out of the way I live. Gayle said I should stop looking for the songs and continue looking for the path. That's what I'm doing. Maybe I'm a bit murky inside so I can't draw that purity to myself that I could if I were clearer. There's no point in longing to be a great songwriter. I should long to be a great meditator. Everything will come out of that."

Ferron smiles at the audience. Her shoulders are less hunched than they were at the beginning of the show. She is more relaxed. "Ummm..." She frowns. "I've got to get 'um' out of my vocabulary. Ummm..." She grins in exasperation, shrugs, as the audience laughs.

"We love you, Ferron!" a female voice calls out from a back row. There is some applause, a few whistles.

Ferron puts her hands on her chest, lifts her eyebrows as if to say, "Who, me?" Then she leans close to the mike and says softly, "I love you, too."

She tunes her guitar. "For this number we need some help on the percussion section. Would you mind playing your car keys?"

There is a hubbub of giggling, talking and jingling as members of the audience retrieve their key rings. Like children, they shake them excitedly.

"Sshh," Ferron says, her finger over her lips. "Not yet." She nods to the drummer, who begins to play an African-style beat on a conga drum. The guitars pick up the beat and add a reggae backbone. The viola comes in with a swirling Middle Eastern melody.

Ferron, strumming her guitar, turns to the audience and mouths, "Now." Suddenly the room fills with a jangling sound of car keys playing a sensual salsa rhythm.

A smile spreads over Ferron's face. She nods her head in time, stamps her feet, sways her hips.

O babe, you are my bellybowl, my soft-shoe shuffle
I come behind, I follow whole, for me there is no other.

©Ferron, Nemesis Publishing

On the musical break, the viola soars, teases. The jangling of keys rises to a joyous fever. There are hoots from the audience. Ferron grins. The audience dances the song with her.

More than anything else, Ferron's songs are poetry. "I see myself as a poet-singer-songwriter who is trying to work with words in a diligent way. It has always been my desire to get the right word next to the right word. Part of the intimacy that people sense in my

songs is my intimacy with words." As she says in "Almost Kissed":
"O I admit that I hold to words, I hold them tight/I've known colder comfort in the night."

Critics invariably praise the subtlety and power of her lyrics. Ronni Lundy, of *Tune In*, said her "delicate and deadly lyrics...eat away at the surface of things, exposing the bare structure beneath." Other reviewers have compared her to other poet-songwriters, especially Bob Dylan, pointing out similarities in the tough, questioning attitude of their songs, the sharp, verbose poetry and the sense of politics that transcends a particular movement. But Ferron's effect on the listener is not like Dylan's. Writing in *Rocket*, Rebecca Brown said, "When you meet Bob Dylan down one of your emotional dark alleys, he knifes you in the back, kicks you in the face and asks if you want a little more. When you meet Ferron down that same awful alley, she gives you a cup of coffee and sits with you while you sip it in the dark."

Ferron herself says, "When I first heard Dylan I was moved by the lonely voice that uses dogs and people and streets and time. I felt less lonely as a writer; I saw that somebody else had a green sky. But when people began to compare me to him, I thought, 'How can they do that when there's no women in his songs except women he's leaving or fucking, women he can't value?'"

Ferron's poetry invites other comparisons. Don Shewey said in *Rolling Stone*, "Ferron writes of love with the relentless introspection of Leonard Cohen....(Their) songs are so full of emotional incidents that you wind up living with them awhile." One critic pointed out that she shares a narrative lyric approach with Bruce Springsteen. Among Canadian women singer-songwriters, Jane Siberry most closely resembles Ferron with her imagistic, sometimes obscure lyrics.

Many of Ferron's songs, like Marie-Lynn Hammond's, explore the disappointing aspects of love, the failure of love to completely fulfill a person. Ferron takes an unidealized view of relationships, neither minimalizing the pain nor sinking into self-pity. She rarely writes about the euphoria of romance. "I experienced that once. I'm too cynical to write about it. I'm not interested in analyzing it. If I did it would be critical and pessimistic because I think that falling in love is like falling out of yourself. I hope it never happens to me again. I don't want to lose myself that much. I write with a pair of scissors, but there's no scissors at that stage of infatuation. I wouldn't want to tamper with that moment because I'd have to cut it up. Besides, it's a momentary feeling that will cut itself up. I'm more interested in when people are a bit off, after the idealistic time, when it's all weird and the ideals crash and you feel you have nothing. I want to say, But you have that and that. It's not what you thought you wanted, but it's real, like the roots of trees."

Even Ferron's titles suggest unfulfillment. In "Almost Kissed" she expects nothing more — *"Not surprised to find me lonely now"* — and even welcomes her aloneness — *"I say hello there brittle and bone/For sure you must be my home."* "Rosalee," which she says is a metaphor for freedom and dependency in relationships, describes a woman who expects too much of love:

> *Rosalee, you tried too hard again*
> *Your stride stumble you down*
> *The horse of love you tried to rope again*
> *In just your cowhide gown.*
>
> ©Ferron, Nemesis Publishing

She consoles Rosalee: *"Don't it make you think that maybe/You're okay alone?"*

"Who Loses," a slow ballad with a heavy, almost dreary waltz-time tempo, speaks of a failed relationship: *"Some loving is torture/ It seems ours is not the way,"* and concludes with a phrase reminiscent of Dylan's "Don't Think Twice, It's All Right": *"Take everything/But don't take my time."*

For Ferron the essence of love is autonomy: mutual respect and caring between people without dependency, possessiveness, domination and loss of self-hood. Nowhere does she express this more clearly than in "Our Purpose Here":

> *It's a woman's dream this autonomy*
> *Where the lines connect and the points stay free*
> *We said passion as an open sea would only haunt you. . . .*
> *I've got memories in the quiet heat*
> *When our words were trim and our hope was neat*
> *We said our purpose here was to be complete*
> *With "I want you."*
>
> ©Ferron, Nemesis Publishing

"I cried my eyes out when I wrote that song, for not being there," she says. "I've been trying to be there ever since, trying to learn that love is not something you have in your pocket."

Ferron is a lesbian, a fact that she doesn't hesitate to make public. She writes love songs to and about women, but she feels that listeners sometimes read too much into the lyrics. "I have a benevolent spirit around me that I'm always writing to. In some songs it's confusing whether I'm writing to a lover or to that benevolent energy." And even where lesbian references are intentional, her homosexuality is secondary to her art. "I never went on a stage to sell lesbianism," she says. In the *Village Voice*, Kate Walter agrees: "Ferron has never been a lesbian-feminist writer — rather, she's a songwriter who happens to be gay."

51

She has always tried to make her songs universal, not only subject to lesbian identification and interpretation. According to the *Boston Phoenix*, she is succeeding: "She makes it clear that lesbian relationships are different from heterosexual ones. At the same time (she) opens up her love affairs to the scrutiny and understanding of nonlesbians...by relying on...images of trains and roads and mountains that everybody understands, rather than the moons and circles and such that have become part of a more exclusively feminist vocabulary."

Yet she has encountered a kind of reverse discrimination from within the lesbian movement for that very universality, for not taking a more vocal stance on her sexual politics. Some gay women have criticized her, for example, for not stating explicitly in "Satin Blouse" that the lover is a woman.

As well, she has at times fallen into disfavour with some feminists. Early in her career she played at the Women's Coffee House in Vancouver, an all-women's club that admitted men only one night a week. Ferron felt that her music was for both men and women; she wanted to perform to mixed audiences and she wanted men to join in singing songs like "Testimony." But some radical feminists in the audience opposed this, and boycotted her show. "I thought I'd be ruined," Ferron says. "But I knew that the only solution is to keep playing, keep trying to reach people. We can't let politics dictate the art."

Gradually the women accepted her view and returned to her audience. On the whole, however, the feminist and lesbian communities have been a major source of support for Ferron, giving her love and respect.

When Ferron recorded *Shadows on a Dime*, she considered using an all-woman band, but while figuring out what kinds of musicians she'd need, realized that she wanted players who sounded like her regulars: a drummer who'd sound like Glen Hendrickson and guitarists who'd sound like Brent Shindell and Brett Wade. "I wanted to play with my guys. Why should I have somebody who *sounds* like them when I can have *them*?" So, again pushing politics aside, she concentrated on making the best music she could, and used "her guys."

Ferron has always maintained that her music is for everyone, not only women. "My music doesn't exclude anybody. One of my dreams is that some men, not knowing I'm gay, will hear my music and like it. Then if they find out about me, every time they say 'bloody dykes' they'll be talking about me. Maybe they'll change that attitude." Indeed, many men are among her fans — including one unlikely male who approached her after a show in Boston. A large, husky, bearded biker, he wore black boots, chains and tattoos. "I just wanna talk to you," he said in a gruff voice. Ferron was terrified. She recalls, "I didn't know what was going to happen. But he just touched me on the shoulder and told me how much he liked 'Ain't Life a Brook.' He started to cry. I stood there and held him and cried with him. He said, 'I've never cried, but when I heard that song, I cried.' He was really sobbing. He said, 'I want to feel and I want somebody to believe that I can.' I felt very touched."

Incidents like that reassure her that her music is reaching beyond a lesbian or feminist audience. "Sometimes I think I was made to write for men. For women my music is an identification, but for men it's a breakthrough, a freedom. In a way, men have been ripped off. They've never been allowed or learned how to have their feelings. They've turned to calcium inside. The line 'Men who easily cry' in 'It Won't Take Long' expresses what I wish men could achieve. That would be their gift to themselves and our gift to them — to have the fullness of all of their humanness."

Achieving this fullness is the essence of Ferron's most political song, "It Won't Take Long," which grew from a dream. "I saw a necklace of people linked around the world, holding candles." The song calls for a humanist revolution in which capitalism will yield to art, and human values will sweep away oppression and greed. This tune captures the rage of songs like Rita MacNeil's "Angry People in the Streets," but like Bob Dylan's "The Times They Are A'Changin'," its message is couched in spiritual, utopian terms rather than concrete political phrases. From the song's genesis in a dream to its poetic evocation of the revolution, this is metaphysical politics.

But liberation is not easy: the song contains a dialogue between the skeptic, who fears and doubts the coming change ("I don't think I can be a part of that"), and the visionary, who welcomes it ("Don't you want to see yourself that strong?"). The skeptic's voice chokes on fear; the visionary's voice scolds, teases and finally exults. Ferron says the two conflicting voices "are both honest parts of me." Speaking with the skeptic's voice, she says, "I'm a pessimist. I think we've missed the moment described in 'It Won't Take Long,' when we were all supposed to stand up and say, No! We didn't do it." She pauses. "Gayle says it hasn't come yet," she adds with a hopeful sigh.

The drum begins a fast, insistent rhythm like a train barrelling down the track. An expectant sound. The viola joins in with sharp, staccato notes scratching against the drum beat. There is tension in the music, something held back, held down — something powerful. Ferron nods her head in time, taps her feet. Her face is grim.

Strumming the guitar, she leans into the mike and sings in a low, gravelly voice.

*They said some men would be warriors and some men
   would be kings
And some men would be owners of land and other
   man-made things
And false love as the eternal flame would move some to
   think in rings
And gold would be our power and other foolish things.*

On 'things' her voice takes a slow slide down the register, ending in a half-spoken growl. The viola refrain becomes a lyrical, drawn-out wail. Ferron distorts her face as if in fear. She whines:

What has that got to do with me?

Then her face softens as she demands:

You mean to tell me that's all?

The viola returns to its staccato accent. The drum continues its insistent rhythm. The guitars play stinging electric riffs. The feeling of expectation intensifies: the song seems about to explode.

Ferron puts down her guitar and removes the mike from the stand. Knees bent, moving in almost tribal motions, she dances around the stage. She gestures, points, snaps her fingers, grimaces. The hard edge in her voice gradually smooths out. At the last verse she stands still. One hand raised, she sings with all the music in her voice:

*We are children in the rafters, we are babies in the park
We are lovers at the movies, we are candles in the dark. . . .
We are words not easily spoken, we're the deeper side of try
We are dreamers in the making, we are not afraid of "Why?"*

©Ferron, Nemesis Publishing

The final 'why' begins low, then moves upward through the scale to end in a triumphant shout.

If Ferron often writes about the losing side in life and love, her music also expresses an acceptance of whatever happens. At times this sounds like mere resignation, as in "Snowin' in Brooklyn." At other times she displays bemused acceptance of life's unexpected turns, as in "Shadows on a Dime." And at other times it's self-acceptance: "Proud Crowd/Pride Cried" she says is "about a hard person whose ego is rendered gentle. It's about shedding the false and defensive pride and hurt and anger that starts to solidify and traps something gentle and generous. I realized that I no longer needed the hardness which at one time had been useful. I wanted that hardness to stop."

The song moves slowly through time like a boat through water, with a melody that laps like waves. Ferron sings it almost mono-tonally, as if holding the emotion in check. For the "I" in the song, insight comes *"with the shock of the knowledge/That I often have needed something out there to blame."* The insight leads to change:

I give up my fisted touch, my thoughts strung like fences
My totem-pole stature, body chipped to the bone
I'm nobody's saviour, and nobody's mine either
I hear the desert wind whisper, "But neither are we alone."

The song finally arrives at self-love: *"I am looking for something outside of forgiveness/You might call it the jewel of the crown."* Ferron says, "That song is the deepest prayer I've ever felt."

Ferron's music is a mixture of country, folk and rock and roll. The country influence comes from her childhood, which sparked a continuing love of the form. But Ferron's country songs are not ordinary heart-on-the-sleeve-in-waltz-time ballads. "The Return," she says, is almost a play on the genre, with its country-style harmonies and instrumentation used as a setting for ideas about spiritual communion—ideas not usually expressed in country music. Her melodies tend to be spare, circular and repetitive, a backdrop to her voice and lyrics, rather than the main focus. When she composes, the melody emerges with the voice. "Re-viewers have described a haunting sound between the guitar and my voice. They move along together. I try to get the guitar sound that my voice, with its limitations, can sit on. It's all one thing."

Ferron has been both fortunate and wise in gathering around her musicians who respect and understand her music and give it a sensitive interpretation. In addition to her band, she has recently been accompanied by Novi Novog, a Los Angeles violist she met in 1982. "I fell in love with that viola," she says. "Novi has created a musical base for me to get stronger in. I have the words but she has so much music in her. She brings real music back into my life. I'm trying to take care of an emotional landscape. She helps take care of it musically. She makes music that expresses the emotions of the song. The audience's mind can relax, and so can I. I don't have to do it all myself."

Ferron's truest musical vehicle is her voice, a rusty, flinty alto that is sometimes smooth and clear, sometimes raspy and cracked. It is a ruthlessly honest instrument whose rough-hewn quality evokes comparisons with Dylan, Cohen and Springsteen. A re-viewer in the *Boston Phoenix* wrote, "Listening to her is like studying your face in a magnifying mirror: pores become volcanoes, and every scar is as ragged as the Rockies.''

Ferron shades her singing with whisperings, croaks and half-spoken lines. She sometimes runs words and phrases together without pausing between lines, bending and stretching words over the edge of the beat, pulling the listener into the next note, the next thought, deep into the song. She says this is not deliberate, but results partly from her early bilingualism, partly because she relives each song as she sings it. ''Sometimes I get teased about my syntax, about how the words come out, but those words are coming from somewhere else. They're pushing their way out. Each time I sing my songs I end up in a different place from the last time I sang them. When I was younger I'd sometimes cry while singing 'Ain't Life a Brook' — it was too hard to go there. But over the years it smoothed out, and I'd hear my voice not jerk through the lines, but pull right through.''

If it is hard for Ferron to go there, it is sometimes difficult for her audiences as well. Rebecca Brown, of the *Rocket*, said, ''Part of the time — when she's singing rebellious love songs like…'Bellybowl' — you feel like everyone in the world is drinking a beer and we're all pals and buddies and slapping each other on the back and we're gonna get by, by God. Then another part of the time she's singing you this song, slowly carefully pulling out your guts, just stretching them out of you and you're… the only person in the whole fucking world.''

Ferron succeeds by being herself. The audience senses her honesty and respects the vulnerability she exposes. Her stage presence — indeed her whole life — is a mixture of cynicism and child-like naivete that makes the audience want to take her to their collective breast and reassure her that they respect and love her, that her secrets are safe with them. And indeed, Ferron's gradual awareness of this was responsible for her transition from a shy, mumbling folksinger to the self-assured performer she is today. ''When I was younger I was so afraid of the audience because I needed their love so much,'' she says. ''It took me a long time to realize that they did love me. Now I like to let the audience know how much power they have. I've said in shows, 'I'd look really dumb if you weren't here.'''

Once Ferron began to gain confidence in herself as a performer, she entered a phase in which she used the audience's response as an ego rush, as a way to validate herself, in a sense substituting audience love for self-love. After a while she realized this was dangerous. ''I had to give up my ego as an entertainer. Eventually I learned to let it go. I got rid of my old expectations, the myths about myself which I was trying to fulfill through my performances.

Now I don't have a lot of illusions about what I'm going to get or going to be. I've learned to accept what comes with the work, not struggle with it or abuse it, just let it be."

Traces of her old shyness still show onstage. She delivers anecdotes in a self-deprecating way with a hint of "will you still love me after you know this about me?" At the 1987 Vancouver Folk Festival, she was slated to follow the Oyster Band, a high-energy English folk-rock band that had the audience on its feet. She was planning to play a quiet, introspective set, accompanied only by Novi on the viola. "I said to Gary (Cristall, Folk Fest director), 'What are you trying to do to me?' He laughed and said, 'I call this the Stan Rogers memorial spot. I want to prove to you once again that intelligent writing can follow Christ, and also that the audience is very intelligent.'" Nine thousand people gave her a standing ovation.

Ferron bears a great sense of responsibility toward her listeners. "They honour me, and I honour them," she said in a radio interview. "The more I dare to give, the more they dare to give. By the end of the evening we've had some kind of a conversation. We've gotten to know each other a bit."

Not only gotten to know each other, but fallen in love. In *Valley Women's Voice*, Kathleen Moran said, "Some critics have called her rapport with her listeners a 'mystical union'... there is also an element of sensuality involved. (She) treats her audience as if we were, collectively, her lover." Ferron agrees. "I can feel love from the audience. I feel their utmost respect. They're so kind and patient, like a really good friend. I want to thank them, to repay them through my music."

A line from "Proud Crowd/Pride Cried" illustrates Ferron's attitude toward her career: "I like to think I never was one for the hoop anyway." With the success of *Shadows on a Dime* and growing recognition in both Canada and the U.S., she no longer sings in small houses, but fills large concert halls, including a sold-out show at Carnegie Hall with Holly Near in 1987. The hoop of major record contracts and large-venue touring beckons. But Ferron and Gayle refuse to jump through. They will continue to produce records independently and advance her career slowly and carefully. "There's always a price," Gayle said in a radio interview. "We decide what prices we want to pay. There are too many bodies strewn along the road of the music industry."

Ferron is terrified at the thought of being suddenly packaged and thrust into the glare of fame and stardom. Besides, she doesn't think it would work. "What would a major record label do with me, anyway?" she says with a grin. "I want to keep my own value system, go at my own pace, let my music develop in its own time.

The goal isn't stardom. The goal is to live an honest life in tune with your feelings, a life that is completely true, with no contradictions. I like to think that when Gayle and I are old we'll know that, given a choice between selling out to fame and fortune in its most seductive form, and staying on the path, we stayed true, even at the cost of being poor and ridiculed. If, by becoming successful, I've lost some of those things, I don't know how much I'll have gained.''

So she conducts her career according to her own needs as a person and an artist, not the demands of the public or the industry. In early 1986, following extensive touring after the release of *Shadows on a Dime*, she was exhausted, unable to write, and felt estranged from her friends. She decided to take time off from performing and traveling. As she told Tom Harrison in the *Province*, ''I needed this time to establish a new base to work from. A mental base, a spiritual base, an emotional base. To meet *me* again, to find out what I care about. Because when you're touring everyday you don't have time for that.'' Except for a few concerts in 1986 and 1987, she remained out of public view, going into seclusion in Mexico for part of that time. Many people warned her that taking so much time off would be unwise for her career, but Ferron kept her goals in sight: ''I don't want to make records more than I want to make me human.''

At the same time, she and Gayle are aware of the enormous value of the American music market. In 1987 she received (by lottery) one of 10,000 ''green cards'' issued by the U.S. government that permit foreigners to work there. She decided to move to Sante Fe, New Mexico. Just before leaving Canada she said to Tom Harrison, ''I have mixed feelings about moving. I'm Canadian; I'll never be an American. At the same time, I'm not attached to the concept of borders when it limits people. On some level I see the move as an auspicious gift—it's always good artistically to be in a new environment. I'm going there to see if I and Sante Fe can have an emotional, artistic and spiritual exchange. It's a leap into the unknown.''

Meanwhile, Ferron concentrates on writing and singing with truth and vision. Beyond that, what comes, will come. ''I always thought I'd be a waitress, so my success seems like an incredible gift. I've already received more than I ever, ever imagined was possible. The isolation of my childhood is broken. My silence is gone.''

The band leaves the stage. Only Ferron remains in the pool of light. Resting her elbows on her guitar with neighbour-over-the-back-fence familiarity, she gazes levelly at the audience. "If I'd known before I started writing songs that I'd end up singing certain ones 250 times — " chuckles from the audience — "in six months" — laughter — "I might have done something else." Hoots of laughter and applause.

Smiling, she shrugs her shoulders. "Oh, well." She begins to finger-pick a gentle refrain, a circular melody. The audience applauds in recognition. Ferron nods, then closes her eyes.

> There's godlike and warlike
> And strong like only some show
> And there's sadlike and madlike
> And had like we know.

All through the song the audience listens attentively, like children hearing a story they know by heart. Then on the last verse everyone joins in.

> And by our lives be we spirit
> And by our hearts be we women
> And by our eyes be we open
> And by our hands be we whole.

There is a moment of total silence. Then applause, whistles, cheers. Ferron's smile is a mixture of shyness and delight. "Thank you," she says, holding out her hands to the audience. Then she walks out of the circle of light.

Marie-Lynn Hammond

La tête anglaise, le coeur français

**"I do what I want to do, and if I don't make it, that's OK.
When I'm on my deathbed I'll be able to say I did what I did
from the heart and I'm proud of it."**

Beautiful Deeds/De beaux gestes:

A musical play in two acts by Marie-Lynn Hammond

CHARACTERS
Corinne: a Franco-Ontarian woman about 60
Elsie: an English-Canadian woman in her late 50s
Marie-Lynn: their granddaughter

SETTING
Ottawa and Montreal

TIME
For Corinne and Elsie, 1944 and 1945. For Marie-Lynn, the present.

*Curtain rises. Marie-Lynn is centre stage. Corinne stands stage left,
Elsie stage right.*
*Throughout the play, Corinne's and Elsie's speeches are directed to
the audience. They share the stage but do not hear one another.*

61

MARIE-LYNN: *(sings)*

Perdu sur une mer vaste et profonde
C'est pas qu'il manque de côtes pour atterir
Mais me voici encore entre deux mondes
Je me demande comment il faut choisir

Car j'ai tête anglaise, j'ai le coeur français
Pris au milieu, entre les deux, je voyage sans fin...
L'âme en conflit, toute ma vie, me voila triste marin.

(Adrift on a vast deep sea
Shores there are a-plenty, though I do not land
For I am caught in the gulf between two worlds
Never knowing which I must choose

With an English head and a French heart
I am trapped in the middle on an endless voyage
Conflict in my soul all the days of my life
I am a sad sailor.)

*M*arie-Lynn Hammond lives alone in an older home in one of those Toronto neighbourhoods where nearly every block boasts a heritage house set discreetly back from the maple-lined sidewalk. Well, not quite alone — she shares the house with an eighteen-year-old calico cat who leaves no doubt who is mistress of the place. She is a slim woman with short, straight brown hair and green eyes. Not twinkly, joking eyes; mysterious eyes that glimmer with privacy and introspection. Both onstage and off, she dresses with simple elegance in clothes falling somewhere between *Harrowsmith* and *Vogue*: bold colours, sweeping lines, loose-fitting tops, tapered slacks. A silver Haida pin on her lapel, perhaps, and a single thin silver bracelet. Marie-Lynn describes herself as a ''serious cat aficionado and horse nut.'' Urban life, she says with a sigh, has made it impossible to fulfill the latter obsession.

Prologue

ELSIE: *Imagine, my first grandchild! My love to all of you. Oh Barney, just one thing — I'm feeling ancient enough as it is these days, so I want you to promise me something.*

CORINNE: *Imagine, ma fille, là là, j'ai quatorze petits-enfants qui vont m'appeler "grand'mère"!*

ELSIE: *Don't let her call me grandmother!*

CORINNE: *Marie-Lynn??*

ELSIE: *Marie-Lynn??*

62

Marie-Lynn Hammond was born in Montreal in 1948, the eldest of three daughters. Her English Canadian father came from a well-to-do, upper-class, Protestant background, her French Canadian mother from a large, working class Catholic family. Both families opposed their marriage. When her father announced his engagement, his mother said, "Take that French girl out if you like, but do you have to marry her?"

There was no obvious clash of cultures in Marie-Lynn's home, no name-calling or assertions of superiority. But in subtle ways she knew mistrust and prejudice on both sides. "My English grandmother was too gracious to let her anti-French feelings show. She treated my mother nicely, but with a certain reserve, as if she considered my mother's people just slightly beneath her. But the French relatives were just as disapproving in their own way. They didn't like our anglo-sounding name. And the fact that my father didn't accompany the rest of us to church didn't sit too well with them."

Then there was the question of language. "My father spoke a little French, but it didn't occur to him that the language of the family should be anything other than English. Partly this was unconscious anglo arrogance, and partly the prevailing attitude of the time — the man was head of the household, so his culture would naturally be dominant. My mother went along with that. She only spoke French to my sisters and me when he wasn't around." Hammond learned French first and picked up English at the age of three. At four, she was completely bilingual.

The French-English split followed her from home to school. In what may have been an attempt to appease both sides of the family, her parents sent her to English Catholic schools. She tried to hide her French background, but in French class her flawless accent was a giveaway. Her classmates teased her and called her names.

Later in life Marie-Lynn realized that the French-English issue was more than a matter of language or religion, more than being called "Frenchie" or "Brit." She understood that it had to do with social class, economic clout, politics and power.

In retrospect, her dual heritage has served her well. It gave her fluency in both languages, respect for both cultures and an understanding of the unique balancing act that is Canada. But it also gave her confusion and conflict, a feeling of belonging in neither culture. This division has been central to her identity as a person and has become a major theme in her work — one that she explores in her play *Beautiful Deeds/De beaux gestes*. The play examines the lives of Hammond's two grandmothers, Elsie Hammond and Corinne Allard. A third character is Marie-Lynn herself, the singer, who acts as a bridge between the two women and the different cultures they represent: "My emotional journey in the play — and in life — is finding a way to resolve the two solitudes within myself."

Act 1, Scene 2

CORINNE: *I warned Thérèse. When she came to me with her big news — she's in love, she's fiancée with some young pilot, imagine-toi donc, they want to get married tout de suite. "Thérèse," I said to her, "ce jeune homme-là, Barney-euh-Hammond: y'est anglais, ben OK. Mais — Protestant! Your father there, he's going to — "*
"Mais maman," she says, "weren't you ever in love? What about when you married Papa?" "Ecoute, Therésè," I said to her, "l'amour — that's a luxury I could never afford. Don't forget, before I met your father, I was a widow with no money and two little babies!... Moise, he built me a nice big house, I had a maid, and he let me buy lots of pretty dresses too.... But he lost his money and had to sell the store, then the house.... I have to work like a slave to feed and take care of everyone, because, oubliez-pas, Moise he gave me eight more babies! So maybe he bought me a piano, but he sure didn't leave me much time to play!

Barney Hammond, Marie-Lynn's father, was a flier in World War II and in peacetime became an air force officer. As a result the family moved every year or so to different towns and air force bases all over Canada and England.

Her song "Down at the Station" explores the rootlessness and aggression of military life. A steady beat seems to hold back the underlying tension in the lyrics; only rarely does Marie-Lynn's voice or the synthesizer break through the veneer of control in a burst of anger. Just as the Hammond family learned not to identify with a place or make close friends, the song warns that the soldiers and officers must *"learn not to get too close, learn when not to talk."* In peacetime the men's lust for war is unsatisfied: *"The biggest tease of all...you spend your whole life cocked and ready/But you never get to shoot for real."* Frustration leads to drinking to *"keep you from thinking too much at night about what you did all day."* Rage is vented against the family: in the song the daughter pleads, *"Oh, Papa, can't you see we're not the enemy?"* The real danger, Hammond is saying, is that militarism becomes the soldiers' identities.

Military themes are not new in folk music. Dozens of songs, from

65

Woody Guthrie's "If I Had a Hammer" to Bruce Cockburn's "If I Had a Rocket Launcher," expose the horrors of war and extol the glories of peace. For Marie-Lynn Hammond, with her air-force-brat insight, militarization is not an abstract evil, but a personal issue that has been with her since childhood. She is currently writing a play about growing up on an air force base and about militarism in society.

Neither of Marie-Lynn Hammond's parents was musically inclined. "They're both tone-deaf," she says, laughing. "My mother sang traditional French Canadian songs and lullabies to me slightly off-key." There were few records around the house and little exposure to music. Perhaps it was her French grandmother, Corinne Allard, who loved to sing (on key), who sparked Hammond's interest in music. As a young child she begged her parents for violin lessons. "I don't know why on earth I wanted to play the violin. I drove my parents crazy until I got the lessons—and then, when they gave in, I drove them crazy for the two years that I played." As a teenager she listened to the popular music of the '60s: folksingers like Ian and Sylvia ("a great influence on me"), Joan Baez, Bob Dylan, and Peter, Paul and Mary, plus rock groups like the Doors and Jefferson Airplane.

In the late '60s, while attending Carleton University (B.A., English), she noticed that everyone was playing the guitar. "It seemed accessible. You didn't need formal lessons to learn to play. I thought, Why not?" She taught herself some chords and learned others from friends, although, as a left-handed person playing right-handed guitar, she found the instrument difficult. She now describes herself as "an adequate guitar player, but nothing special." Many years later she took piano lessons, but discontinued them to concentrate on playwriting.

Her voice is largely untrained as well; it wasn't until she'd been performing for ten years that she took singing lessons. She sings in the contralto range with a murky shading and a slight roughness. Her voice isn't flashy or dramatic, not polished or canary-like. It doesn't dazzle you with its technical prowess. But it has an appealing honesty that makes you listen closely to the words. It's pretty but not only pretty: it's the voice of a woman who means more than she says. Hammond doesn't belt out songs like Heather Bishop or Connie Kaldor, but sings evenly with subtle inflections. The nuances are more important than the volume. She plays out her songs like fishing line, forcing you to grab hold and pull yourself hand over hand back to the source to discover their full import.

Hammond is diffident about her vocal ability. "I don't have a huge range, as compared to somebody like Connie Kaldor." Despite vocal training she's been unable to significantly expand her range. This frustrates her, as does the lack of a natural vibrato which she says makes her voice sound emotionally flat. "It's hard to make the emotion sound in my voice, so I have to live the songs, really give myself over to them to convey the emotion I feel." The critics disagree. One called her voice "a magnificent instrument," and a reviewer in the *Calgary Sun* wrote, "...she has a voice with the range and power to make you think the singer is anyone from a young girl, to a young girl in love, to a woman who has had it with love."

From the beginning Hammond has been more attracted to song-writing than to the instrumental or vocal side of music. Singer-songwriters like Joni Mitchell, James Taylor, Dylan and Simon and Garfunkel impressed her with their poetic crafting of lyrics. Driven by an urge to write, she began to compose songs which she describes as "folky love songs that were very derivative of the popular folk music of the day." While at Carleton she joined her friend Rob DeFries in singing traditional and contemporary folk songs around the Ottawa area. They enjoyed modest success as a campus act, but she was not considering a career in music because she really wanted to be an artist. This, like music, was an interest she had developed on her own with little example or encourage-ment from her family.

In 1970 she moved to Toronto for art school and there met a left-wing songwriter named Bob Bossin who was looking for someone to join him in a folk group. Hammond missed singing with a partner, and agreed to form a duo. In 1973 they added a fiddler and took the name Stringband. At this point Marie-Lynn was still equally interested in art and music.But as the band began to make a modest living playing coffee houses, folk clubs and campuses, she decided to pursue a musical career.

Stringband's repertoire consisted of original compositions (at first, mostly Bossin's), contemporary folk songs, traditional French Canadian vocal and instrumental numbers (which Hammond, the only francophone in the group, searched out), and fiddle tunes. Among them, the musicians played acoustic guitar, banjo, fiddle, autoharp, tambourine, spoons and other percussion instruments. In 1974 they self-produced their first album, *Canadian Sunset*, under what Marie-Lynn calls "primitive conditions." Despite the production quality, it exceeded their commercial expectations and was critically well-received. (Over the years it's sold about 20,000 copies.) Encouraged, they continued to perform and record, releasing *National Melodies* in 1975, *Thanks to the Following* in 1976, *Maple Leaf Dog* in 1978, *Stringband Live* in 1982, and the cassette *Across Russia By Stage*, following a tour of the Soviet Union, in 1984.

Bossin had connections with the university community and was usually able to get Stringband gigs on college campuses. But not always. One summer, when work was scarce, the band busked on a section of Yonge Street in Toronto that had been turned into a pedestrian mall. "I remember one sweltering evening," Marie-Lynn says. "Bob, Jerry the fiddler, and I stood out there on the mall and sang, sweating in the humidity. Afterward we took the loot back to my apartment and counted all the quarters and one-dollar bills. It came to about $20 each—not bad for three hours' work. That was worth four or five meals in a cheap Hungarian restaurant."

Then there was Stringband's feud with the Mariposa Folk Festival. The band applied to play there two years in a row and were turned down. The third year they enclosed with their application an invitation which Hammond had printed in fancy calligraphy: "Stringband's Third Annual Application to Mariposa—Games & Prizes & A Good Time For All—R.S.V.P." The Mariposa board was not amused. In a letter to the group, they said that Stringband was not traditional enough and, moreover, they weren't a real string band. Later Stringband quoted from the rejection letter on one of their promotion sheets. They never did play Mariposa.

What set Stringband apart from other folk groups of the period was its Canadian identity. In the late '60s and early '70s, Canadian nationalism was growing and being expressed, expecially in literature and theatre. But it was less evident in popular music. Some well-known performers like Gordon Lightfoot, Ian and Sylvia and Murray MacLauchlan had recorded songs with Canadian references, but most bands either weren't interested in Canadian subjects or feared that singing about them would make their music less marketable in the U.S. and abroad.

Stringband disregarded these qualms. Both Hammond and Bossin were nationalists with a strong interest in presenting music by and about Canadians. They searched out material by Canadian songwriters, both traditional and contemporary (they were one of the first groups to perform Stan Rogers' songs), included both French and English songs in their repertoire, and wrote tunes that explored Canadian history and politics. Of the fifteen songs on National Melodies, for example, three are traditional French Canadian, two are fiddle tunes from the Maritime region, one, written by Angèle Arsenault, is made of nonsense syllables that approximate the Mic Mac Indian language, and two of the four original songs have Canadian themes.

"Mrs. Murphy," co-written by Bossin and Hammond, is a slow waltz ballad about the struggle of Canadian farm families to resist selling their land to large "agri-business" corporations. Mrs. Murphy is not presented as a hero. On the one hand she wants to keep the farm; on the other she is tempted to yield to the per-

suasions of the company men who *"come round with the seasons...*
with an offer that's good for us all," and follow her children to the
city, where they've *"traded the land for a catalogue vision/Of a*
modern apartment right out of their dreams." Her ambivalence makes
her real, and helps even the most urban listener identify with farm
families in this situation.

Stringband's Canadian identity was, in retrospect, a bold affirm-
ation of cultural nationalism. Marie-Lynn and Bob focused their
repertoire on bilingual, Canadian-oriented material — not because
it was commercial but because that was the kind of music they
cared about. And the unexpected happened: Canadian listeners
responded. Audiences were first surprised and then delighted to
hear music about themselves. While the band didn't achieve
stardom, they did receive critical acclaim and generated a loyal
following from coast to coast.

But Hammond wasn't entirely happy in Stringband. The group's
identity had always been more Bossin's than hers, especially in
political content and musical style. After a while she wanted to
push the band toward jazz and swing, but Bob resisted, favouring
the acoustic folk sound they began with. "By that time I was writing
more," she says. "I had a clearer sense of what I wanted to say
and how I wanted to say it. I resented the way Bob changed my
songs to fit his conception of Stringband's style." In 1978 she left
the band and formed her own group which performed a mixture of
swing, country-rock and jazz material, both original and borrowed.
The following year she released her first solo album, *Marie-Lynn*
Hammond, and followed it in 1983 with *Vignettes* (seven songs she
wrote as part of the play, plus four others), and, in 1985, the
cassette *Impromptu*.

Act 1, Scene 5

ELSIE: *I was at a Victory rally one fine spring afternoon....*
There were speakers and a band, but best of all, they
had a fellow flying an airplane.... First, he did all
sorts of fancy loops and rolls, swooping low over the
crowd and making people duck and cry out, but not
me. I was mesmerized! Couldn't take my eyes off the
plane, or the pilot. And then damned if he didn't fly
right under the Interprovincial bridge! God, what
nerve! The next moment he was a tiny speck in the sky;
and suddenly, more than anything, I wanted to be up
there with him, climbing and climbing, free of the
crowd, free of the pull of the earth. I watched until I
couldn't see him anymore, and I swore right then and
there that I would learn to fly too.

MARIE-LYNN: *(sings)*

> *Over Queen Charlotte Sound*
> *The lichen-covered rocks below are grey and rust-brown*
> *Foam on the water like filigree*
> *Sun scatters sequins of gold on the sea*
> *And Ted with the log book and his head bent down*
> *While I'm holding her steady over Queen Charlotte*
> * Sound.*

Love is important in Marie-Lynn Hammond's music, especially on her first solo album—all stages of love, from early romance to the hindsight that follows the demise of a relationship. In "Maverick Gleam" she questions her new amorous feelings:

> *Maybe it's just a mirage that I'm seeing, some maverick gleam*
> *A trick of the way light falls in a dream*

and she opts for faith: *"But I think finally this time/I can trust the view."*

More often, though, she writes about the failure of love, about not trying hard enough or trying too late to make a relationship work. The "I" in her songs is often a person who wants to love and be loved, but who refuses or is afraid to commit herself or relinquish her autonomy. In "Houdini and You and Me" she confesses:

> *Whenever somebody gets too near*
> *You lose your nerve and disappear...*
> *I've been pulling that same old trick for years*
> *Masters of the great escape are we*
> *Houdini and you and me.*

"Loving and Losing" is a slow, gentle waltz in which the violin refrain adds a tone of elegance amid despair, as if the partners are determined that if their relationship must fail, it will fail with style.

> *Yes we're loving and losing in three-quarter time*
> *Such a gracefully sad affair*
> *So strike up the music, now pour out the wine*
> *And show me someone who's never been there.*

Some of Hammond's songs describe lovers out of sync with one another. "But for the Timing" is a song of regret for missed connections:

> *I'm sorry for whatever came between*
> *Sorry for the love that might have been*
> *But for the timing.*

Oh the things we keep, the things we throw away...
Oh the things we feel, the things we never say...
Oh the things we learn, the things we learn — too late.

"Le coffre à jouets" ("The Toy Chest") adds Marie-Lynn's music and lyrics to a poem written by her mother to create a song full of longing and loss. Her mother opens an old, forgotten toy chest and finds dolls, marbles, books and

Un rayon de soleil, une poignée de tristesse
Adieu mes petits, adieu mes amours, adieu jeunesse.

(A ray of sunlight, a handful of sadness
Farewell, my little ones, farewell my loved ones
Farewell to youth).

She sifts through the treasures, finally coming upon an object that symbolizes her life, her marriage and her hopes: *"Et enfin un casse-tête qui manque des morceaux un peu comme entre nous." ("And finally a puzzle with pieces gone missing/Somewhat the way it has been between us.")*

But Hammond's songs are not bitter. Like Ferron, another song-writer whose music often conveys the failure of love, she keeps her sense of humour about her and emphasizes the "almost," suggesting that even the failures are worth the effort. Both songwriters are resigned to the fact that relationships sometimes fail, and determine to find — or create — one that will fully satisfy both partners.

Act 1, Scene 6

CORINNE: *When Jean-Marie was born, it was un accouchement très difficile — very long and very hard. Finally, the doctor left, and I fell asleep, the baby beside me. Sometime later I wake up — no baby! He's gone! Just then I hear noises from downstairs, and I remember, there is a grate in the floor near the bed and I can see through it into the store. Right under is the counter and Moise is behind it. In front of him are the children and three or four customers. And there in the big scale on the counter is Jean-Marie, mon p'tit! Pis là I hear Moise saying — ah, qu'y était fier! "R'gardez bien, mesdames et messieurs, ten pounds and a quarter! And me, I'm seventy-two years old!" Imagine! And me so tiny! I wanted to yell at him: "Garde-le donc, ton dix livres et quart! Me, it almost killed me!"*

71

MARIE-LYNN: *(sings)*

> *Quand j'étais jeune mariée, diddle i don*
> *Mon mari m'a dit: viens ici t'coucher*
> *Pis neuf mois plus tard, voila un petit bébé*
> *C'est une fille? ben oui*
> *Pas un garçon) ben non, diddle i don*
>
> *Pis faut choisir son non*
> *Pis faut l'appeler Marie queq'chose*
> *Marie-Cecile c'est un beau nom*
> *Appelle'la donc Marie-Cecile*
> *Marie-Cecile, diddle i don*
>
> *Marie-Yvonne, Marie-Colette, Marie-Thérèse, Marie-Madelaine*
>
> *Encore une fille? ben non*
> *C'est un garçon? ben oui, diddle i di!*
> *Pis faut choisir son nom*
> *Pis faut l'appeler queq'chose de beau*
> *Appelle-le Joseph Jean-Marie*
> *J'ai dit appelle-le Jean-Marie...*
> *C'est un garçon, diddle i don!*
>
> *(When I was a young bride, my husband said to me*
> *Come along to bed*
> *And nine months later there's a little baby*
> *Is it a girl? well yes*
> *Not a boy? well no*
>
> *So we have to choose her name*
> *And we have to call her Marie something*
> *Marie-Cecile's a nice name*
> *So call her Marie-Cecile*
>
> *Marie-Yvonne, Marie-Colette, Marie-Therese, Marie-Madelaine*
>
> *Another girl? Well no!*
> *It's a boy? Well yes!*
> *So we have to choose his name*
> *And we have to call him something special*
> *Call him Joseph Jean-Marie... It's a boy!)*

Since her first solo album, Marie-Lynn has concerned herself less with romantic love and more with the idea of autonomy. "I've made a conscious effort to broaden my themes. Since 1983 I've written only one love song. My more recent work has been much more about family, women's lives and sexual politics."

This shift in focus reflects her identity as a feminist. "Feminism encouraged the development of a lot of women musicians, including me. The women's movement has been the source of most of my strength and my ability to do what I'm doing. It helped me realize that I had a right to do this, that my concerns were just as important as anyone else's. As a feminist whose feminism has been growing and maturing, I've moved away from the narrow romantic world of 'my romantic feelings' and 'his romantic feelings' because I feel it's important for women to view themselves autonomously and not always in relation to a man."

No one could be more independent than the calico cat in the jazzy tune of the same name. Hammond sets up this slinky feline as the model of cool, sexy womanhood:

> *Whatever she does she does just as she pleases*
> *And nobody can break her heart...*
> *The toms... don't mean a damn thing to her*
> *Well she'll pick them over when she's in the mood...*
> *She ain't afraid to be rude...*
> *I sure could use a lesson from her.*

Marie-Lynn further asserts her independence in "Girl Who Can't Say Yes," a jaunty ragtime number which she calls a "social and personal satire":

> *And though I've had offers to tie the knot*
> *And walk down the aisle to the altar*
> *I must have some block, for when I look at that knot*
> *It seems to turn into a halter.*

"Second Fiddle Rag," a lively tune with Stephane Grapelli-style violin breaks, tells the story of a woman who asks her husband to teach her how to play the fiddle. His response is, *"Forget it, Sugar, that'll be the day,"* and informs her that a woman's place is at home. But the plucky heroine is undeterred. She secretly buys a fiddle and teaches herself to play. Soon she lands a job in a jazz band and, after her husband leaves her, supports herself with her skills. The setting is five decades in the past, but the message is now.

Hammond believes that music can be a force for change. "Songs can help people understand things about themselves. People take home the spirit of the music." A special interest of hers is peace.

"Distant Early Warning Line" expresses the loneliness of working on the DEW Line in northern Canada.

> *He sits in front of the radar screen*
> *Watching the signal, watching the planes*
> *Go pulsing across, leaving their tracks of light.*

The work insinuates itself into the workers' consciousness until it becomes more than just a job:

> *He's scared that he might be caught now*
> *'Cause some find their way back but some do not.*

Most of Hammond's political songs express their messages subtly through image and metaphor, but some, which she calls "ditties," present her stance with humour. "The ditties are fine for rallies but they're not art," she says. One of these ditties is "Radiation," a gospel-style number in which she and her backup singers alternate calling out "Radiation!" with as much fervor as if they were shouting "Amen!" She describes the mutagenic effects of radiation: *"I woke up this morning/I counted my toes/My God, I had sixteen,"* and advises everyone to *"start a demonstration at your local hydro station."*

Marie-Lynn frequently plays at rallies and benefits for such causes as environmental protection, women's issues and peace. "In Toronto whenever a group needs a singer for a rally they usually call Nancy White or me," she says with a laugh. "We keep running into each other at these things." Indeed, the pile of invitations to play at benefits grew so large that she had to write "Not Another Benefit." A desperate caller implores her, *"Situation's critical, she said you're quite political/And feminist, and always play for free."* Her reaction: *"Oh no, it's a benefit, not another benefit/And none of them benefit me."* In the end, she goes broke because she's so busy doing benefits that she has no time for paying gigs: *"We'll have one more benefit — this time for me."*

Hammond's keen wit also comes through in "Canadian Love," a lightly trilling waltz which laments the difficulty of pursuing passion in northern climes:

> *Oh Canadian love, Canadian love*
> *It's either forty below or it's ninety above*
> *And though it's hard to be yearning*
> *When you're freezing or burning*
> *Like the dollar we keep falling in Canadian love.*

And in the boogie-woogie tune "Leave Room for the Holy Ghost"
she recalls a highlight of her Catholic education. A nun, speaking
to the girls before a big co-ed dance, prohibits them from wearing
patent-leather shoes, lest the boys see the reflections of their under-
wear in the shiny surfaces. Then she cautions:

> *The Devil can't stand a good Catholic girl*
> *That's the kind he likes to tempt the most*
> *So remember when you're dancing close*
> *To leave room for the Holy Ghost.*

Act II, Scene 8

ELSIE: *The next day Ted just turned up out of the blue, took
me by the arm and said, "Come along, Elsie — today I'm
giving you your first flying lesson." And I should have
learned then, shouldn't I? But I didn't. Why? Because
I made the mistake of falling in love with my instructor.
And once you fall in love with a man, they'll never
teach you anything. First they get critical, then they
lose their patience, and finally they become so insulting
that you're scared they won't love you anymore and
you cry out, "Stop! You're right. I'm slow, I'm stupid,
and we needn't do this again, ever!..." I never did get
my license. I never did fly solo. Because once I was
with Ted I didn't care to anymore. I mean, why go
alone when you can go together? Never did fly solo.
But really, I've... no regrets.*

MARIE-LYNN: (sings)

> *Elsie was a beauty and she was a wild one*
> *The only time she pleased the family*
> *Was when she married a banker's son*
>
> *He enlisted in the Great War*
> *There wasn't time to stop and grieve*
> *Elsie knit sweaters for the men at the front*
> *And slept with the ones on leave...*
>
> *Hand-tinted photograph of Elsie in her younger days*
> *They say my sister's got her eyes*
> *But I've got her willful ways*
>
> *Restless spirit, dance, dance on, maybe if you'd lived today*
> *All that drive and passion might have found a way*
> *Elsie won't you dance.*

Most of Hammond's songs begin as a lyric idea: an image, a
phrase, a character in a situation. She fools around on the guitar or
piano, trying to find the notes or chords to express the concept.
Words and music usually emerge together, although sometimes she

comes up with a set of lyrics to which she adds music later. The essence of songwriting for her is crafting the lyrics. Like Ferron, she is known as a songwriter who creates evocative, poetic images that linger in the mind. She loves to play with the meaning, rhythm and musicality of words. The "Calico Cat" has *"three-coloured crazy-quilt fur/She slinks and creeps, she leaps and teases."*

Hammond is not content with the obvious word or the easy rhyme. "I try not to write one-idea songs. I like my songs to have layers of meaning so you can come back to them and keep finding something new." As well as being lyrically complex, her songs are often rhythmically varied, changing tempo to emphasize moods like rain squalls and sunshine alternating in the prairie sky.

An eclectic stylist, she writes and performs simple folk-style songs, ballads with elaborate orchestral accompaniment, traditional French Canadian music, ragtime, swing, jazz, blues, gospel and rock and roll. She favours minor keys, which suit her voice. Influenced by her French Canadian heritage, she likes to include unusual percussion—spoons, chimes and wood blocks. On her records she builds a full, rich sound with piano, electric guitar, violin and smooth vocal backup. She uses a synthesizer judiciously.

Hammond's talent is boundless, and she thrives on writing and singing, but her commercial appeal has always been limited. Her live solo act has remained relatively unknown. For her first solo tour, she and her band piled into a van and headed west, hitting every snowstorn along the way. During a white-out in Minnesota she thought, "Is this worth it?" Certainly financially it wasn't: she managed to pay the band but had to use her own savings to finance publicity and van repairs. Most of the folk clubs and coffee houses had been converted to disco halls, and there were few venues interested in booking a bilingual act whose music ranged from '20s swing to '70s jazz. "We were too pop for the folkies and not pop enough for the rockers. And some people expected me to still sound like Stringband."

As well, Hammond found she was ill-suited to being the leader of a band. She lacked experience and interest in booking gigs, keeping a payroll and attending to administrative details. She also found that some men in the band resented taking direction from her. "Behaviour that's assertive in a man is considered aggressive and ball-breaking in a woman. At one rehearsal the bass player and I were disagreeing about an arrangement. Suddenly he exploded into yelling, 'Who do you think you are? You're just a woman!' I was shocked. It struck me as a misogynistic outpouring that had nothing to do with the music. I didn't doubt my ability to lead the band, but I found the tension unpleasant and wearing."

Nor did her albums achieve commercial success. Critical success, yes. Estelle Klein, former artistic director of the Mariposa Folk Festival, called her "one of the best contemporary singer-songwriters in Canada." But her first record got lost in the disco-dominated music scene of the late '70s. *Vignettes*, which she put out at her own expense, received good reviews but almost no interest from radio stations and record stores, and sold about 3,000 copies. *Impromptu* fared about the same. Her music is simply too original, thoughtful and eclectic to fit the popular music market. Most radio stations (except the CBC) have ignored it. "Radio stations don't want to play stuff that's not available in the record stores, and record stores don't want to carry stuff that's not being played on the radio," Marie-Lynn says. "It's a perfect catch-22."

In this situation, many singers try to sound more "pop," angling for a commercial breakthrough. Connie Kaldor, for example, used a rock approach on her second album in order to increase radio play and reach a wider market. Marie-Lynn Hammond, though, has been steadfastly unwilling to compromise. Although she would like more recognition and feels that she deserves it—"Some of my songs are as good as anything that's been written in Canada"—she doesn't waste time feeling bitter. "My voice doesn't lend itself to pop styles anyway, and I'm too intelligent to be satisfied writing monosyllabic songs about love." More important to her than commercial recognition is the desire to write according to her vision. "I could choose to go commercial, make all the compromises in the world, and still not make it. Then at the end I'd have nothing to show for it, not even self-respect. I do what I want to do, and if I don't make it, that's OK. When I'm on my deathbed I'll be able to say, 'I did what I did from the heart and I'm proud of it.' That's what matters."

Hammond realized, soon after releasing her first album, that it would be difficult to succeed commercially as a solo musician, so in 1980 she rejoined Stringband on a part-time basis with the understanding that Bob was the sole leader—a compromise she was willing to make in order to assure some income while leaving time to work on other projects.

One of these was the play. For some time Marie-Lynn had felt limited by the three-minute song and had been searching for a new framework, a different format, the right climate and soil for growing her ideas. Around this time she saw Ann Mortifee's show *Journey to Kairos*, a suite of songs linked by narrative passages. Soon after, she began to write the song "Elsie," and the song inspired her to explore the differences between her two grandmothers. She realized that the musical-suite format would be the perfect vehicle for this idea. But she'd have to make some alterations. "My voice isn't as strong or versatile as Ann's, so I figured I'd need more of a framework to hang the songs on — something like a series of dramatic vignettes connected by music."

With a Canada Council grant to assist her, Hammond began to write *Beautiful Deeds/De beauz gestes*. True to the heritage of her two grandmothers, she wrote dialogue and lyrics in both French and English. "It's interesting that I composed most of the English songs on the guitar and most of the French ones on the piano. To me the piano has a romantic, classical sound that goes well with the French language." In addition to her own songs, she altered some poems written by her grandmother and her mother and set them to music.

Writing the dramatic portion of the play was difficult. Marie-Lynn collected anecdotes from elderly members of both families, and examined old photographs, poems and journals. She researched fliers and bush pilots, World Wars I and II, and Canadian history of the period. But even after her thorough research, the dialogue didn't ring true. After much thought she figured out why: in real life the two women had nothing to say to one another. In fact, they met only once, on the eve of their children's wedding, which they both opposed. Hammond realized that they would speak to her, their granddaughter, so she made herself the structural link between the grandmothers. She rewrote their dialogue as monologues which they deliver to her or to the audience, and made their meeting the climax of the play. Her own character, the granddaughter, responds to them in song, creating the illusion that she is having a dialogue with them. At first she saw the granddaughter's role as secondary to those of Elsie and Corinne. "But gradually I understood that I was the apex of the triangle."

After being workshopped several times, *Beautiful Deeds/De beaux gestes* received its first full production in 1984, co-produced by Theatre du P'tit Bonheur, an Ontario francophone company, and Manitoba Theatre Centre. Later it was produced by the Blyth Festival and was nominated for Best New Play at the 1984 Dora Mavor Moore Awards. The three-woman cast took the show on tour in the fall of 1987, performing at the National Arts Centre in Ottawa, Persephone Theatre in Saskatoon and other theatres in southern Ontario and Montreal.

Because *Beautiful Deeds/De beaux gestes* is bilingual, it tends, as Marie-Lynn says, "to fall through the cracks. Francophones don't want to hear English, and anglophones don't want to hear French — especially in western Canada." Still, the play has been enthusiastically received almost everywhere. "There was one night in

Winnipeg when the audience was totally with us. They got all the nuances, subtleties and humour. They were laughing almost before we got the punch lines out." Toronto audiences were particularly fond of Elsie's speech about not learning to fly solo because she fell in love with her instructor. "That night there must have been a lot of women in the audience who had tried to learn to drive with their husbands," Marie-Lynn says. "At that line they burst into applause."

Critics have lauded the play. In the *Winnipeg Free Press*, Reg Skene said, "...the grandmothers emerge as powerful feminine figures, attempting to work out private destinies in a world which scorns such attempts....In the climactic scene of the play, in which they finally meet face to face...a full range of irony and dramatic excitement is realized." Doug Bale, in *The London Free Press*, said, "The originality of the show's concept speaks well for the head on her shoulders, and the best testimonial to her heart is the delicacy with which she manages to touch the hearts of her audience."

Beautiful Deeds/De beaux gestes has introduced Marie-Lynn Hammond to a new aspect of performing: stage acting. It isn't a role that she relishes, but one she accepts. "I'm not a natural performer," she says. "The fact that I was originally interested in art shows that I'm a bit of an introvert. Over the years I've learned to be a good performer, but I'll never be the type to embrace the limelight. I like to let my work make the statement, instead of putting the focus on me." Onstage she comes across as friendly and in command of her material, but slightly reserved. She treats the audience intelligently and respectfully, presenting her material in a forthright manner, rarely hamming it up or spoofing onstage. "The creative act is a private act between the muse and me. I'd be happy to make albums and write plays and not perform at all. Performing isn't where my gifts lie."

Act II, Scene 10

ELSIE: *Well, it's clear from the letter that arrived last week that my arguments had an effect — the effect of a red flag on a bull. "Dear Mother" — hmf — he knows I prefer Elsie. "Dear Mother: Frankly, I'm surprised at the vehemence of your reaction. You spoke of differing backgrounds and cultures. You imply that her family has no position, no money, no style. What about you and Ted — talk about opposite worlds!" But that was different! Ted and I, we created our own!*

CORINNE: *"L'amour, Thérèse," j'ai dit, "that's not the only thing to think about in marriage." "Yes, but what about the others," she says. "Yves, Cecile, Madelaine, Yvonne —*

they all married for love!" OK, OK, c'est vrai, ça, but at
least they fall in love with Catholics!"

MARIE-LYNN: *(sings)*

He had twelve days leave when she met him in Montreal
They courted and then there were married
He wore his uniform
She wore her grey silk suit and a hat with a veil
Her mother shook her head and said, You hardly know
    the boy
But it was the spring of '44, it was such a crazy time
And he seemed so brave, so full of glory
And his eyes shone blue as the sky
When he talked about flying

"Oh flying
Well the Hurricane is a damn fine plane
And I wish you could see all the boys and me
Doing loops and dives in tight formation
Chasing the wind like eagles in the sun."

At first, during the play, we see only the contrasts between Elsie and Corinne, but gradually the things that tie them together become more apparent — their humour, their loveless marriages and moments of passion, their strength. Although her grandmothers were limited by the social values of their day, they are not passive or weak. "Some radical feminists have accused *Beautiful Deeds* of not being a feminist play because Elsie and Corinne live so much through and for their men. Yet most women — and I — agree that this is a true reflection of how it was. And even so, these two grandmothers still had a strength and independence of spirit which could inspire me and pave the way for women today."

Elsie's speeches and Marie-Lynn's lyrics convey the longing to seek adventures, test oneself, take chances, experience a heightened reality. Marie-Lynn herself is not driven by the quest to fly as her father and grandmother were. "But in a way, the life I've chosen is parallel to flying," she says. "Being an artist has an element of risk. I don't conform to tradition; I'm always pushing at the limits around me. I can understand Elsie's and my father's urge to soar above the clouds, even though I have no desire to do it literally."

Ultimately, *Beautiful Deeds/De beaux gestes* isn't so much about Corinne and Elsie as it is about Marie-Lynn Hammond, and about her attempt to reconcile French and English, Catholic and Protestant, wealthy and poor, upper class and working class. Her quest leaves her divided between her English head and French heart — but not entirely. Everything that separates Corinne and Elsie is finally transcended by their affection for their children. In the end they unite, whether they realize it or not, through the love that will produce their granddaughter.

Beautiful Deeds/De beaux gestes was a major turning point in Marie-Lynn Hammond's career, marking the transition from music to theatre. Her second play, "White Weddings," is scheduled to be produced in the fall of 1988 by Factory Theatre, directed by her mentor Jackie Maxwell. Hammond describes the play as "a black comedy about family relationships."

Has Hammond abandoned music? No. She still writes songs and does the occasional solo gig at a folk club or music festival. She performed at the Calgary Winter Olympic Arts Festival, and recently sang with Bob Bossin at a Toronto cafe, doing old String-band tunes. "It was a bit ragged, but the old stuff is so burned into our brain cells that it just takes a few days to get them into shape," she says with a laugh. She and Bob are now planning Stringband's 20th anniversary for 1990. "Music isn't dead yet for me, it's just in a resting phase." The literary side is clearly ascendant now.

From singing with a band to a solo career, from writing songs to writing plays or hosting CBC Radio's "Dayshift" during the summer months, Marie-Lynn Hammond has never been one to do the same thing for long. Like the early Canadian explorers, she is too restless to remain in charted lands, always testing herself against the unknown. "I want to learn new things, so I have to be willing to take chances. It's hard but it's worth it."

Act II, Finale

MARIE-LYNN: *(sings)*

> After childhood faded, like a distant lullaby
> The world broke into two with no clear path in view
> But now time has turned me circles
> Turned me round again to see
> That two voices can become a single heart that speaks
>   as one
> And their songs still echo down through time to me.
>
> Oui j'ai la tête anglaise, j'ai le coeur français
> Ici au milieu, entre les deux, je suis mon destin
> J'ai la tête anglaise, j'ai le coeur français
> L'âme appaisé grace au don du passé
> Me voila enfin fier marin

> *(Yes, I have an English head and a French heart*
> *Here in the middle, between them, I follow my destiny*
> *With an English head and a French heart*
> *My soul is soothed thanks to the gift of the past*
> *And finally I am a proud sailor.)*

Sylvia Tyson

Bridge Over Musical Generations

"I like my music to work on the personal level of small, daily statements of people's lives. If you can make a difference there, you'll make a difference on a larger level."

1963. *Sylvia Tyson is twenty-three years old. On the cover of Four Strong Winds, Ian and Sylvia's second album, she sits on a sand dune, head turned to the side, gazing at the ocean in the distance. Her long brown hair blows in the wind; wisps of hair stream across her face. In a flowered smock dress belted at the waist, like that of a Grecian maiden, wearing not a trace of makeup, she has a softness about her, the softness of femininity and youth. Facing the horizon, she seems full of idealism, as if looking beyond this troubled world to a better place.*

1987. *Sylvia is forty-seven, and she's talking to a journalist at 21 McGill, an elegant women's club in Toronto. Strains of a Bach concerto mingle with the murmur of conversation and the clatter of bone china, while a waiter hovers nearby with a silver tea service. Sylvia's still-long, thick brown hair is now flecked with grey. She wears eye makeup, lipstick, stylish blouse and skirt. Bronze earrings dangle from her ears, a matching watch is pinned to her blouse. There is a hint of wariness and weariness in her eyes, but when she smiles, the years slip away. This is the same Sylvia Tyson who sang so earnestly more than two decades ago.*

When talking about Sylvia Tyson, one is tempted to call her legendary, "the grande dame of Canadian women's music." But that would consign her to the past, a dusty relic in some Folk Music Hall of Fame. That's not only unfair, but also inaccurate, since she's still an active and popular songwriter and performer. Her career stretches over nearly three decades and encompasses two separate phases — her partnership with Ian and her solo work. Counting Ian and Sylvia records, she's made seventeen albums. She's had her own television show. She's hosted several TV specials. Her career has been — well, legendary.

Almost everyone in this book, when asked to name their early role models, gave the same list: Joni Mitchell, Buffy Sainte-Marie and Sylvia Tyson. Not that younger women have copied their style of music or subjects for songwriting or way of conducting a career; each forged her own path. But all of them were aware of Joni's, Buffy's and Sylvia's music. All of them knew those three were out there, working, singing, doing something true. And now the middle crop of musicians — people like Heather Bishop, Connie Kaldor, Ferron, Nancy White and Marie-Lynn Hammond — are the role models for women like Lucie Blue Tremblay, Jane Siberry and Tracy Riley. Tyson will always be a star in the firmament.

At the age of fifteen, Sylvia Fricker decided to be a musician. That was no surprise. Her mother, a classically trained pianist, taught music, played organ and directed the Anglican Church choir in Chatham, Ontario, where Sylvia was born in 1940. Her mother's favourites were Mozart, Chopin, and popular singers of the '30s and '40s like Rudy Vallee. Her father loved Bach's organ music and Gilbert and Sullivan. He was an instinctive self-taught musician. During the Depression he demonstrated pianos for Heinzmann during the day and played nights at Amy Semple McPherson's mission — "before she hit the big time," Sylvia says, breaking into one of her pealing laughs.

Tyson's mother tried to teach her the piano, but the arrangement didn't work. Her mother hired a teacher, and Sylvia studied for many years, but never mastered piano. "It's not my instrument. I don't really have an instrument. Playing doesn't come naturally to me. I regret that I don't play an instrument better than I do. It's limiting. But you can learn to work with your limitations and to stretch them."

Apart from the music her parents played and listened to, Sylvia's main source of music was rhythm and blues from the Detroit radio stations. "My friends were crazy about rock and roll artists like Buddy Holly and Little Richard, and so was I. Plus early Elvis and Jerry Lee Lewis. There was something genuine about their music. You could tell it was second nature to them. They grew up with it and had a real feel for it. That's what I've always looked for in music. I get very impatient with contrived stuff." She heard country

music on the radio, too, but didn't pay much attention. "My parents and friends considered country music low class, working class. I didn't consciously listen to it but it was there and it influenced me. I didn't really appreciate it until I started listening to Appalachian music a little later." At the time, CBC Radio broadcast a few folk music shows hosted by Alan Mills and Ed McCurdy, but she found the three-chord guitar arrangements simplistic and didn't listen much.

In her grade ten poetry book, Tyson found several old English ballads with written music. She figured them out on the piano, and her taste for traditional music was born. She combed the local library for English and American folk songs from the Childe, Sharpe and Lomax collections, and was particularly keen on Appalachian music. This thorough grounding in traditional music turned out to be an advantage later when she arrived in Toronto to begin her career. "Most of the other folksingers had learned their material from the half-dozen or so folk albums available, but I had a much larger repertoire of different kinds of songs they didn't know."

All through her teens, Sylvia sang alto in the church choir, learning to sight-read and harmonize. She wanted to play the guitar, but had no teacher. She devised her own method of playing by tuning the strings in a chord and barring up the neck of the guitar. "I figured out that if it was a chord down here, it'd be a chord up there, too," she says with a laugh. Without realizing it, she'd adopted a style used by many of the old blues players — musicians much in favour among young Toronto folksingers she met a few years later. (To her surprise, instead of looking down on her for not knowing how to chord a guitar, they were impressed by her technique. "How'd you learn to play like that?" they wanted to know.)

Tyson had no one to emulate. Except for Alan Mills and the Travelers, who were known nationally, the Canadian folk scene of the late '50s was regional, consisting mostly of traditional material performed locally. "I probably didn't know there was any Canadian music at that point," she says. Even in the States, the folk revival was not yet underway. Although the Weavers and Malvina Reynolds were well-known, Sylvia didn't hear them until she moved to New York. "The closest thing to a role model I had were the black male artists I heard on Detroit radio."

Tyson made careful plans to launch her career. "I didn't want to plunge myself into the music scene and fail because I wasn't well-prepared." After graduating from high school she worked in a jewelry store in Chatham for a year to save money for her move to Toronto. During that time she made several trips to the city to check out the folk music scene. She introduced herself to club owners and met other musicians, including a tall fellow from British Columbia, seven years her senior, named Ian Tyson. Ian later recalled her as "a loner, original, very introspective, small town, green."

Sylvia moved to Toronto in 1959. She launched her career at the First Floor Club, and soon was singing at folk clubs and coffee houses around the city with a repertoire of traditional English and Appalachian songs, tunes by Woody Guthrie and Burl Ives, and spirituals and work songs of the American south. For a while she performed alternate sets with Ian Tyson at the Village Corner Club. Ian had grown up listening to blues, jazz, country, and rock and roll, and had played in a Vancouver rock band before coming east. He featured tunes by Big Bill Broonzy and other blues artists. He'd been in a duo with singer and actor Don Franks, but they had parted, and Ian was looking for a female partner. Impressed by Sylvia's voice and her knowledge of music, he suggested they try working together.

"Our tastes in music were quite different. We always had a lot of arguments about our material," she says. "But I think the tension made the music interesting. When there's too much agreement, the music gets bland." At first they sang Sylvia's Appalachian songs because their voices suited the material. "Besides," she says, "no one else was performing that kind of music, so our show was unique."

Ian and Sylvia performed in and around Toronto for the next couple of years. "We were the 'Kansas City Stars' of Toronto," she says, referring to a popular Roger Miller song about a young man who becomes a star on his home turf but is unknown elsewhere. By the early '60s they were aware of the contemporary folk music scene growing in the U.S. "I was blown away by Joan Baez's first album — not for what was on it but just because it existed. It was a folk record by a contemporary of ours and someone had put it on a label and was selling it. There were signs of life."

In 1962 they decided to go to New York, the centre of the folk movement. Ed Cowan, a friend and business student at Ryerson, declared himself their manager. The three of them knocked on the door of Albert Grossman, who managed such luminaries as Odetta and Bob Gibson. They auditioned right in Grossman's office overlooking Central Park. "He liked us — but he'd just signed this new trio we'd never heard of, and he didn't have time to take on another group." The trio turned out to be Peter, Paul and Mary.

Eventually Ian and Sylvia did sign on with Grossman. When they began planning their first record, they chose a label by looking at the album jackets of Joan Baez and other folk artists. "We were keen to record on Vanguard because it was *the* folk label, the prestige label." Grossman tried to talk them out of it, arguing that Vanguard lacked business sense in marketing folk music, but they insisted. Grossman negotiated their first record contract, and the album *Ian and Sylvia*, a collection of traditional songs, came out on Vanguard in 1962.

Grossman's warning proved true. "Vanguard was a disappointment," Sylvia says. "They didn't understand distribution and promotion. Their idea of a major ad campaign was to put an ad in the *Evergreen Review*. They'd started out as a classical label and assumed that records would sell themselves because of their quality. That worked with classical music, but not with popular music."

Nor did they make much money from their concerts. Most club owners took advantage of the image of folksingers as poor, itinerant minstrels, and paid minimum fees. During the early '60s they played coffee houses and folk clubs in New York and Toronto, commuting between the two cities. In New York they usually stayed at the Earl Hotel. "It had a kind of seedy charm. There was a piano bar with a pianist who'd been there since the '40s. But it was affordable, and the plumbing worked — that was the main thing."

This was the heyday of the folk revival. They added colleges to their circuit and hung out with many soon-to-be-famous musicians like John Hammond, Jr. and Bob Dylan. "We'd never heard of Dylan. He was a slightly overweight guy who was sleeping on people's floors, bumming drinks and writing songs. We figured if he could write songs, anyone could," — a peal of laughter — "but we soon learned not to try to keep up with his output." Alongside Dylan, Hammond, and Simon and Garfunkel, they played at Gerde's Folk City. Monday night was Hoot Night and the stage was open. "It was a great place to sing because the audience was very much of a listening audience. They came to hear the music. Later, when I got into country music more, I had trouble getting used to singing in country bars because the people were so noisy. I was spoiled by starting out in a place like Gerde's.

"The owner of the club was a Greek man named Mike Porco. He didn't know much about folk music but he must have realized that it was the coming thing. Also, it was what he could afford — he didn't pay very much. I remember how he mangled everybody's name. He called us Inos and Sylvia, and introduced Lightnin' Hopkins as Lightningus Hopikinisus."

Over the next several years Ian and Sylvia played all over North America, and released twelve albums — seven on Vanguard, two on MGM, one on Ampex and two on CBS. For the first few years, their partnership was strictly professional but they became romantically involved, and married in 1965. Their only child, Clay, was born two years later.

Folk festivals were big in the '60s. Ian and Sylvia played at Mariposa several times, but had difficulty getting booked at Newport. Several Newport organizers had been active in the folk music movement of the '40s, when political songwriting grew out of union struggles. They favoured musicians with strong political views—people like Tom Paxton, Odetta, Pete Seeger, Dylan and Joan Baez. Ian and Sylvia's music just didn't fit. "It never occurred to us that music was political. It wasn't that our politics were wrong, but that they weren't stated." When rumours about the Newport decision reached them, they took it philosophically. "We knew we were good and that people wanted to hear us. We figured that eventually audience demand would bring it about." It did, along with some helpful persuasion by Albert Grossman and Peter Yarrow who was on the Newport board of directors.

When they finally did play Newport, they were well-received by audiences who knew their material and enthusiastically sang along. Their second appearance at the festival occurred the same year that Dylan went electric. "The audience was booing and hissing, Pete Seeger was walking around backstage with tears streaming down his face. But I don't think the reaction was so much a result of his going electric as a result of the band he used. They were all good musicians, but he threw them together at the last minute and they didn't have time to rehearse. If the band had been tighter, there probably would have been a different reaction."

Ian and Sylvia's repertoire evolved into a mixture of traditional ballads, spirituals, country tunes, songs by other contemporary songwriters and, later, their own compositions. Their sound was characterized by clean vocal harmonies and simple but tight instrumentation provided by Ian on guitar, Sylvia on guitar or autoharp, backed by bass, percussion and pedal guitar on some of the country numbers. Ian almost always sang lead, and the blend of his deep, strong baritone with her lighter, smoky alto was a perfect match. Their smooth sound was similar to Peter, Paul and Mary and the Kingston Trio. Ian fronted the group, talking to the audience and introducing songs. "People always assumed that because he did the talking, he also chose and arranged all the music, but actually we did that together."

After a few years of performing other people's material, they began to write, and their first songs will probably never be forgotten. Ian's in 1963 was "Four Strong Winds," and about six months later Sylvia wrote "You Were On My Mind." In subsequent years their albums contained a greater proportion of original songs and less traditional material. The Tysons rarely wrote together.

"In all our career we collaborated on maybe three songs," Sylvia says. "We used each other as a sounding board but kept our song-writing separate." Ironically, their growing productivity as song-writers caused problems. "We each wanted to incorporate our own songs into the show as solos. The new songs pushed out ones that were familiar to people who liked to hear the two voices together. It became a logistical problem."

While she and Ian were still performing as a duo, Sylvia decided to make a solo album of her original material. Ian produced the record, called *Sylvia Tyson*, for Capitol Records in 1975 and two years later he produced her second solo album, *Woman's World*, also on Capitol. Their last joint album came out in 1974. Four years later they split up professionally and maritally. Sylvia has released three more solo albums since then: *Satin on Stone* in 1978 and *Sugar for Sugar, Salt for Salt* in 1979 (both produced by Don Potter on Sylvia's Salt Records label), and *Big Spotlight* in 1986 (produced by Ian Thomas on Stony Plain Records).

Becoming a solo musician was difficult for Sylvia. "I'd never fronted a band or talked to the audience much. More important, I had almost no experience singing lead. I'd always sung harmony. I spent years adjusting my voice to Ian's. I wasn't quite sure what my voice was or what it could do. Yet I was a star with a reputation to live up to. I had a lot to learn in a hurry." She learned on the job, touring with her band, The Great Speckled Bird, all over Canada and the United States, performing in every kind of venue from concert halls to country bars. Once they played in Calendar Bay, Ontario, home of the Dionne quintuplets. There was no piano in the club, and the manager was nowhere to be found. It turned out he'd won a big national lottery and was on his way to Ottawa to collect his money. "We searched the town for a piano. Finally we found a bad Wurlitzer electric piano at the Legion Hall."

Around the time she went solo, Sylvia met Paul Mills, a CBC Radio producer who was planning a weekly folk music show called "Touch the Earth." When Mills offered her a position as the show's host, she began a stint that lasted nearly six years. Tyson's job was to interview musicians, introduce documentaries by freelance journalists, and introduce live and recorded musical selections. Although the show did not have a mandate to concentrate on Canadian music, it did include a high percentage of Canadian content. "Part of the reason 'Touch the Earth' was so popular was that we searched out musicians all over Canada. It wasn't just a Toronto show," Sylvia says. She and the production crew traveled a great deal, working with local producers and local musicians. One season "Touch the Earth" crossed Canada by rail, recording music on the train and in studios along the way. A very young and inexperienced Heather Bishop made her national radio debut in a station stop in Winnipeg.

Tyson's radio work soon led her to television. For two years she hosted "Heartland," a documentary program produced by CBLT, the Toronto affiliate of CBC. "Heartland" portrayed the people and the regions of Ontario. Sylvia went on location with the production crew, interviewed the subjects and introduced the segments on the air.

In the last years of Ian and Sylvia's partnership, and in Sylvia's solo career, her music began to go country. After hosting "Heartland," she joined "Country in my Soul," a weekly CBC show featuring Canadian and American musicians. Although her official job was performer and host, she also chose the material, band members, musical director, guests and costumes, and usually rewrote the script. Tyson performed a few songs on each show and sang duets with the guests, including Emmylou Harris, Kris Kristopherson, Janie Fricke and Doc Watson. Her experience on "Country in my Soul" led to another job with the CBC, working on the production staff for "Video Hits." Her fascination with television continues: she was an executive producer of the "Ian and Sylvia Reunion," broadcast on CBC in 1987, she's submitted a proposal for a TV game show, and she's working with a friend on a comedy-drama series. "I now see TV and music as separate but equal careers," she says.

In the early '80s Sylvia expanded her musical and business talents into record production. She produced two albums on her Salt Records label — one for the Jarvis Benoit Quartet and a very unusual record called *Inside Out*, recorded at the Edmonton Institute Maximum Security Prison. She had been playing in Edmonton, and the prison psychologist asked her to give a free concert for the inmates. She said that wouldn't accomplish much except to provide an evening's entertainment, and asked if any of the prisoners played or sang music. Soon she was conducting a songwriting workshop with ten inmates. Some of them had real talent, and she got the idea to make an album of their material. She guided their songs through several rewrites and produced *Inside Out*. The record was critically well-accepted but didn't receive much radio play. "I came out of that experience without any Pollyanna view of either the inmates or the prison system. All those guys were in maximum security for a good reason. But they had something to say and they said it well."

Despite wide-ranging interests, Sylvia Tyson is above all a musician, never wandering far from writing and singing. She doesn't follow a particular regimen for songwriting. "Sometimes I write a song in half an hour and don't change a word. Sometimes

I work on a song unconsciously for a year or more. Sometimes I get an idea and just keep working at it for hours or days until it's finished." She jots bits of writing in notebooks which she reviews from time to time. "I've had ideas that never quite came together until I collected all those little isolated scraps. Then they began to make sense." She seizes inspiration when it strikes. "My friends are used to me turning vague and suddenly tuning out." Usually she writes on the piano rather than the guitar because she can quickly translate the chords in her mind onto the keyboard. "While I'm working out the melody I don't necessarily know what those chords are, I just know what the sound is. I figure out the chords later." Although she has written more than one hundred songs, she says she's never been a prolific writer. "I tend to work to rule. If I have an album to do, I write songs. I use up all the stuff I've been storing in my head. I'm never not writing, I'm just not always writing it down on paper."

Sylvia's best-known songs tell stories, encapsulating people's lives in a few verses. In "Regine," for example, she contrasts two sisters, the beautiful, favoured, irresponsible Regine and the plain, unloved, dependable Ellen. Ellen raises her sister's unwanted children, secretly wishing she were Regine. Another country tune, "Denim Blue Eyes," portrays a couple who had a fulfilling life on the farm (*"Our children were born and they grew like the corn/And our lives were as rich as the clover"*), but were forced to sell their land and move to the city (*"We've come to this place that's worse than any hell/Though they call it the city of angels"*). Now the wife watches her husband fade away: *"Each day I see how his soul is dying/There's pain in his denim blue eyes."*

Tyson's song subjects are changing, though. "I don't write as many story-songs as I used to. I realized that it was a copout because I didn't have to tell people much about myself. *Big Spotlight* (her most recent record) is a very personal album." There is frank self-revelation in the song "Bitter Pride": *"I have pride, bitter pride, with my coffee every morning/And leftover pride for my dinner at night."* "Driftwood" confesses a deep sense of dissatisfaction: *"Like driftwood I'll never reach the shore/... I don't want to drift anymore."*

But Sylvia is uncomfortable revealing too much of herself, so she intentionally blurs the line between biography and autobiography. "A songwriter can disguise intense personal feelings in the character of someone else. That makes writing emotionally-revealing songs easier." Still, disguises go only so far. "Young songwriters often come to me and ask me to listen to their songs. Some of them are concerned that they've revealed too much. I tell them if you're going to worry about someone finding out something about you from your song, you probably should look for another line of work, because you reveal yourself whether you mean to or not. You can't worry about hurting someone else's feelings; you have to do what is necessary to make a good song."

Most of all, Tyson loves to sing about love—all kinds of love, from first romance to last good-bye. *"Oh, I love you/You are my smiling wine,"* she says in "Smiling Wine," and in "Blame It on the Moon" she sings playfully:

> *You can blame it on the moon if you want to*
> *It really was big and bright*
> *And though it gave the whole show an exceptional glow*
> *It was you who lit up the night.*

She also writes about the terrifying rush of love. "Too Short a Ride," which she co-wrote with Colleen Peterson, sounds a bit like Connie Kaldor's "Danger Danger." Love strikes in a "forbidden territory," flashing an alarm: "No safe place when hearts collide." She asks: *"Should we play this painlessly, holding back our hearts/ Or shall we burn our wings like moths around a candle?"*

Like every good country singer, she specializes in lost love. "Trucker's Cafe" tells of a woman who hoped for *"a lifetime of love wrapped in a bundle/And placed in the hands of a man."* But, *"He climbed in his rig and was gone,"* and now *"I'm working from morning till midnight/And weeping from midnight to dawn."*

"Summer Suddenly," which she co-wrote with her son, Clay, (who, not surprisingly, wants to be a musician) uses sand, waves and sun to frame a plea for reconciliation with a lover:

> *Walking the sand alone, hand full of skipping stones*
> *Like throwing love away and giving up yesterday*
> *Changes in you, changes in me, summer suddenly.*

Sometimes Tyson portrays women as strong, independent partners in love relationships. In "Blind Leading the Blind," she refuses to be used by someone who doesn't genuinely care for her: *"You were looking for someone to pull you through/Was I the best friend you could find?"* More typically, though, the woman is the passive recipient, the emotional nurturer, as in "Sleep on my Shoulder": *"In my arms you will find someplace quiet to unwind/ ...Sleep on my shoulder for awhile."* She takes refuge in a relation-ship: *"You are my harbour, my dream of tomorrow, my promise of sunshine, my shield from the storm"* in "Yesterday's Dreams." The message seems to be that a man's affection makes a woman whole; take that love away, and she is nothing, a wreck on love's treacherous shore, until another man comes along and fulfills her again.

"Woman's World" follows childhood into the emotional and hormonal turmoil of puberty and finally into the prescribed role of woman.

> *Woman's world, cooking and babies*
> *Little girls with knowing eyes*
> *Woman's world, caught in a circle*
> *Smaller than truth and bigger than lies.*

There is irony in this domain, a subtle parallel between the security of knowing one's role and being trapped within it. Yet Tyson does not condemn these stereotypes — she merely describes them. "'Woman's World' bothered some women listeners because they thought it was degrading to women," she says. "It discusses women as they are and as they were, rather than as they should be. I make no apology for that. Finally most feminists came around to the idea that it was simply an honest statement about growing up."

Sylvia Tyson grew up before feminism became a significant social force and has never become involved in its struggles, as have most of the women in this book. With the exception of Marie-Lynn Hammond, who started her solo career with a mixed audience brought along from her days in Stringband, all the others here have depended on the women's audience to build their careers. Rita MacNeil started out singing feminist songs to all-women audiences, branched out to bars and folk festivals, and finally, after many years on the circuit, made the crossover to large, mixed crowds. Heather Bishop, Connie Kaldor, Ferron and Lucie Blue Tremblay all began with a core of support comprised mostly of women and have consciously tried (and are still trying) to reach a broader audience.

Sylvia Tyson is different. She had a large, loyal, mixed audience from her earlier career with Ian, and continued to appeal to the same audience when she went solo. As well, her country music made her popular with country fans, already a mixed audience. She never needed the women's movement to build her solo career. "I identify strongly with many feminist goals and ideals but I object to the separation and segregation that feminism implies in many cases. I'm a humanist rather than a feminist. I don't think it's harder for a woman to succeed in music. You're as successful as your talent and ambition make you. Only rarely have I been held back because I was a woman. When Ian and I were each doing shows on TV, the television executives were upset that they had to negotiate separately with me. I asked for a specific amount of money, and they said, 'We've never paid that much for a Canadian female performer.' I said, 'OK, see you.' Pretty soon we worked it out."

Sylvia is grateful for her broadly-based audience. "Many women musicians want to expand beyond the women's audience but are locked in. That audience can turn against them if they attempt to broaden their appeal." Recently Sylvia, along with a woman friend, attended a concert given by her old friend Alix Dobkin, a left-wing feminist lesbian. "My friend and I were the only straight women in the audience. The hall was packed, it was standing room only, but there was a moat of empty seats around us." Afterward, Alix tried to talk her into playing women's music festivals in the United States." Alix said that I couldn't use my men band members. That was my first objection. Then she told me I couldn't sing songs about men. That was number two. Then she said that at one festival where she particularly wanted me to play, the women performers and audience always sleep out under canvas tarps and swim nude in the lake." She laughs. "That was number three—and the end of the discussion."

Certainly Tyson is not anti-feminist. She is an independent woman musician with far-ranging interests and capabilities. But feminism just hasn't been crucial in her life or career, so it is not a major theme in her music. Similarly, she is not a political song-writer. She avoids overtly political subjects, yet she has written songs expressing fervent social idealism. "Freedom Now," a rollicking gospel number, recalls the civil rights struggle of the '60s, but could just as easily refer to personal, psychological freedom: *"Freedom now, just a step away/Don't you wait another day for freedom now."*

"We Sail" is an anthem of hope:

> *We sail and we sail together*
> *The name of our ship is the New Beginning*
> *And our sails are a hopeful colour*
> *Filled with the wind of changing times.*
>
> *We sail and the sea around us*
> *It wanes and it swells as a great heart beating*
> *All the storms of the night are passing*
> *How can we sink when we can fly?*

"In the 1960s everyone believed they could change the world— and they did. Music still serves as a political rallying cry," Tyson says. But she does not see herself as a musical crusader. "I'm a small-p political songwriter. I'm concerned with daily injustices rather than big ones. I like my music to work on the personal level of small, daily statements of people's lives. If you can make a difference there, you'll make a difference on a larger level." One of these small-p issues is Vietnamese war orphans; she recently co-wrote a song called "Bamboo" with Shirley Eikhard and Nancy Simmons. She does her share of political benefits: she sings for Amnesty International and she protests free trade and censorship.

She has a definite Canadian sense of place that's so strong in many of this country's musicians. "Canada has so much distance and space and isolation, such a harsh climate — this shows in the arts, especially music and literature." She points out the small-town life that crops up in her work, the isolation and boredom of "Same Old Thing":

> *Saturday night in a one-horse town*
> *Watching the cars cruising up and down...*
> *Big farm boys in their daddy's trucks*
> *High-heeled girls with their hair pinned up.*

In touring all over North America, she's noticed differences between Canadian and American audiences. "Canadians are more conservative. They don't want you to change. They like to be comfortable with the material and don't like surprises. Americans are less critical of change. They like to hear new songs in new arrangements and are more open to anything you want to do."

Sylvia Tyson has a distinctive voice, hard to describe but instantly recognizable. It isn't clear-as-a-bell like Connie Kaldor's, nor mellow like Anne Murray's, nor throaty like Heather Bishop's. Her voice has a smoky quality, a slight nasality and twang well-suited for country material, and a strong vibrato that gives it a pleasing fuzziness. She has a wide range but is entirely untrained vocally. "I have a flawed voice. There are lots of things I'd like to do with my voice that I can't. But I do have a unique voice — no one else sounds like me."

Tyson is known as a fine stylist. A critic in *Sounds* magazine wrote, "(She) has the uncanny knack of creating or destroying a mood within the space of a few bars; her phrasing is immaculate." Her singing has a refinement and an evenness that sometimes subdues the emotion of a song. No frills. No exaggeration. You can't imagine her slurring words and growling like Ferron, or belting out lyrics as uninhibitedly as k.d. Lang.

But her delivery isn't passionless. The emotion is there, and it shows most on blues numbers where her voice sizzles much more than on the country material. But it isn't her style to shout or rasp or bellow; she wants to ensure that the song works as a musical whole. "I've always loved song arrangements, instrumental lines interwoven with the lyrics and the voice. I try to give songs the treatment they require, rather than trying to mold songs into a particular sound that is 'my sound.' A lot of pop artists do that, and it gets boring."

She avoids repetition by singing a variety of styles. "While singers from the folk period have proven to be uncomfortable with the various shifts in music, Tyson seems to thrive on them," says the *Washington Star*. "She covers country, blues, quasi-cabaret and folk tunes with skill and displays none of the stiffness which infects...some of her contemporaries." To some extent she has had to fight the image of being primarily a country singer. "Because Ian and I did a lot of country material toward the end, and because of my work on "Country in my Soul," people thought of me as only a country artist. I love country music but I don't want to limit myself to it because it can be extremely narrow."

Big Spotlight dispelled any notions of the one-genre singer. Like her others, the album has a mix of styles, though it is best described as pop. She's continuing her eclectic approach on her next album. "I want this one to be less electronic-sounding and keyboard-oriented, more organic, funky and natural-sounding."

You'd expect performing to be second nature for a seasoned entertainer like Tyson. On the contrary, she says, "I'm not a natural performer, although I've learned to be a good one. I didn't go into music out of some need to sing and dance for the folks. I went into it because I loved music and, once I started writing, I wanted people to hear my songs. My ego is wrapped up in my songs, not in myself as a performer. I like presenting my new songs and getting feedback on them, but the romance of the road is gone for me."

Onstage Sylvia dresses in elegant but simple clothes and wears her hair long and straight. Although she generally uses a five-piece band, recently she's been playing with only a bass and a piano, looking for a cleaner, more pared-down sound. Her stage presence is straightforward: little banter, no theatrics, just lots of music. Some musicians perform with a populist attitude, but not Tyson. Nothing in her demeanor suggests superiority—she just exudes specialness, graciousness, pride in having a gift. She is an entertainer, not one of the gang. She respects her audience and commands their respect.

Her professionalism follows her offstage. In 1980, she toured Alberta as part of the Traveling Folk Festival and Good Time Medicine Show. In Edson, she and the other performers were waiting in the hotel until it was time to do sound checks. The tour sponsors asked her to pose for pictures with a local dignitary. She replied that she'd have to change her clothes first—she was wearing jeans. "People have a certain image of me as a performer," she said. "If I go out dressed like this it won't fit their image. I'll disappoint them. Fans don't want performers to look and be like ordinary people. They want them to be special."

Valdine Ciwko, who was on the support crew for the tour, recalls, "At first I couldn't understand why Sylvia wouldn't just go out there as she was. But then I realized that she was right—people *did* have a certain perception of her and would have been disappointed if she didn't live up to it. She had a very clear sense of herself as an entertainer. She recognized the importance of image."

Tyson prefers playing for family audiences in small towns to singing in large cities, where the club scene delivers a more narrow audience. "Playing small towns keeps me in touch with people. I don't shut myself off from the audience. I try to talk to people individually after a show, not just sign autographs." She is gratified when people let her know that they can relate to something in one of her songs. "One woman said, 'My husband died recently. That song you sang made me feel better.' I think of myself as writing songs that people would write for themselves."

Sylvia's solo career has not enjoyed the success of her career with Ian. Her records have done well and she's never lacked for work, but she hasn't become the star that she and Ian were together. She's aware of this, but she doesn't worry about it. She's too busy with other projects to push her music career any harder. She knows that if she compromises—if she adds more glitter, dresses a little sexier, arranges her songs in a more pop-electronic vein, tours more—she could climb a few more rungs on the ladder to stardom. But she's not interested. Ferron's phrase, *"I never was one for the hoop anyway,"* sums up Tyson's attitude toward fame and success. In "I Don't Dance" (from *Big Spotlight*) she says:

> I had a dream late last night
> I was standing alone in a big spotlight
> I heard a voice from way up there
> Saying, 'You'd better dance or you'll get nowhere.'
>
> But I don't dance, I just sing
> No one else can pull my strings
> I just play a little, nothing fancy
> I let my fingers do the dancing.

When the music history books are written, Sylvia Tyson will be remembered not only as Ian's partner, not only as a fine songwriter and singer, but also as one of the pioneers among Canadian women singer-songwriters—a pioneer not in the sense of a crusader for women's rights or a political visionary, but as a woman musician who forged her own career, stayed true to her musical ideals, and kept writing and singing good music year after year. Without realizing it, she showed younger musicians that it could be done. And she's still doing it.

The Colours of the Song

"Performing is my favourite thing....I get on the stage, start the first song, the people put out this energy and before I know it the concert is over and I've had a great time. I've got tears in my eyes because people have been so loving. That magic is precious."

*L*ucie Tremblay wanted something that would set her apart. The name Tremblay is as common in Quebec as Smith is in English Canada, so there was nothing distinctive about her name. But blue was her favourite colour, carrying almost a spiritual resonance for her: "There's nothing better for me than a nice dark blue sky or just to be by the blue ocean... it is a good colour for me." So she became Lucie Blue Tremblay. And she isn't blue in name only; she plays a blue Ovation Adamas guitar, often wears blue clothes, and decorates her curly, shoulder-length brown hair with streaks of royal blue. Now, people remember her name.

There is a twinkle in Lucie Blue Tremblay's eyes, a sense of fun. You sense that she rather enjoys people's surprised reaction— "Blue hair?" Yes, blue hair, and why not? Hanging around with her, you feel like reaching for the can of chartreuse or magenta hair spray yourself.

Whimsy aside, blue suits Tremblay because, for her, colour is emotion, and emotion is the essence of her work. She is inspired to write by strong feelings, and delivers her songs with the same emotion that drove her to compose them. "I'm like a big piece of emotion on two legs," she jokes. There is great warmth in her lyrics and in her singing: you feel the person behind the song and accompany her on an emotional journey to your own heart. For Lucie, blue is not a cool colour; her blues come from the warm side of the spectrum, from the hot blue centre of the flame.

One might expect that Tremblay and Marie-Lynn Hammond, both of whom were exposed to French and English cultures while growing up, would have a great deal in common. But beyond their bilingualism and the fact they sing in both languages, their song-writing and musical styles are distinct. Hammond is the poet, Tremblay the chanteuse. There is a much closer parallel between Lucie Blue Tremblay and Rita MacNeil. The Quebecker and the Nova Scotian share an emotional approach to music. Their songs come from the heart, and so does their singing. Both favour simple lyrics and melodies. And just as Rita sang to herself in the bedroom, Lucie pretended she had a microphone and, imagining herself a modern-day Shirley Temple, sang "On the Good Ship Lollipop" in front of the mirror. "I always knew I would sing," she says.

Born in Montreal in 1958 and raised there, she was the younger of two daughters in a French Canadian family. Her father was a civic worker, while her mother worked as a telephone operator, among other jobs. Both parents loved music; her father's favourite being country music while her mother listened to everything from big band music of the '40s to contemporary pop. "My parents were older when they had me. My mother was 38, my father 43. They enjoyed music of an earlier time, 'easy listening' stuff like Al Martino. They listened more to English than to French music." And both parents were musical, though self-taught. Her father played the guitar by ear. For her mother, music was a serious hobby. She gave accordion lessons while Lucie was a baby, and at age six Lucie very briefly studied piano, voice and tap-dancing at the school where her mother taught (hence the Shirley Temple imitation).

That year Lucie's mother had a respiratory illness and couldn't properly hold the accordion, so she switched to the organ. In the late '60s she started a band with several musicians young enough to be her children. They played French and English top-40 songs and swing classics like "In the Mood" at weddings and parties. Lucie tagged along with the band, often falling asleep in the cloak room of whatever church basement or community hall they were playing in. When she turned ten, her mother assigned her the job of keeping watch over the drummer. "My mother had trouble with some of her drummers. They were often late and irresponsible. At the gigs they drank or chased the girls. One of them tried to teach me the drum part for the slow songs and waltzes so I could

take over the drums and he could go and cruise the girls." She laughs, "My mother went through a lot of drummers." That was fine with Lucie: "I loved to pick up the drum sticks and play. I learned lots of rhythms, so when I was twelve or thirteen I became the band's drummer for a few years." With the staggering pay of $40 per weekend (staggering, at least, for a teenaged girl), she decided that the musical life was definitely for her.

When Lucie was ready for school, her parents decided to send her to an English Catholic school. This was in 1964, before the separatist movement had begun to build wide support in Quebec. "When I was young, if you wanted to become anyone or do anything, you had to learn English. People didn't stand up for French culture so much then. They felt they had to adapt to the English-dominated society. My parents realized that it was important for me to be bilingual in order for me to succeed in Canadian society and to have more choice of jobs and places to live."

Those early school years were difficult ones for Tremblay. "The main problem was that I was raised in one culture, and then placed in a totally different one. Naturally there were language barriers. I didn't understand anything, while the other kids easily understood what the teacher was saying. When I started school I knew how to say 'I understand' and 'I don't understand' in English—that was it. I had to learn English at the same time that I was learning the school material." Later, she wrote the song "Panne d'essence" ("Not Enough Gas") about the abrupt and difficult cultural transition. In the end, her parents' goal was fulfilled: she is fully bilingual. She speaks English fluently, albeit with an accent, and writes and sings in both languages.

The Quebec folk groups Harmonium and Beau Dommage, with their meaningful lyrics, vocal harmonies and acoustic instrumentation, were major musical influences on Tremblay. She also listened to the traditional Acadian music of Edith Butler and to contemporary Quebecois pop chanteurs like Fabienne Thibault, Diane Dufresne and Jacques Salvail. Although she heard Gordon Lightfoot, Anne Murray and Murray McLauchlan, she wasn't aware of other English Canadian musicians such as Buffy Sainte-Marie, Stringband and Ian and Sylvia. At school she joined her friends in listening to groups like the Jackson Five and the Osmonds, while on her own she sought out singer-songwriters like Joni Mitchell, James Taylor, Simon and Garfunkel, Cat Stevens, Loggins and Messina and especially Carole King, of whom she says, "Her songs are strong in the way they're formed, and I think that had a big effect on me."

Lucie is mostly a self-taught musician. As a teenager she took a two-week course in guitar. "I learned 'The House of the Rising

Sun,' 'Fly, Little White Dove, Fly,' and 'Michael Row the Boat Ashore,' and I was on my way," she says with a laugh. That was the extent of her formal guitar training. Everything else she knows on the guitar, she taught herself. She's always had a good ear and a facility in figuring out the chords to songs. While in her teens she heard some Anne Murray tunes on the radio, figured out the guitar part and then sang them with her mother's band. Recently, she taught herself to play the piano. "I can read music a little but I couldn't sit down and sight-read a complicated piece. I can really only play what I've written."

Tremblay's lack of formal training hasn't hindered her. She won a Fine Arts Award in high school for guitar and voice in 1975, and was awarded a college scholarship in music. She started the program, but the Quebec teachers' strike interrupted her studies. As well, the school's emphasis on opera made it hard for her to develop her own kind of music, so she dropped out.

Although Lucie Blue Tremblay has never taken singing lessons, her voice is her strongest musical asset. Writing in *Folk Pressings*, Robert E. Weir called it "a voice that rivals Judy Collins for clarity, power and sheer beauty." She covers a wide range of pitches and shadings, spanning soprano to alto. At times her voice is low and deep, at times soft and high, but always it seems to have a minor shading, a slightly husky, bluesy tone. There is a tinge of hoarseness, sometimes breathy in the lower ranges and tremulous in the higher register, that gives her singing a pleasing sensuality. Her voice has a deepness and mellowness that remind one of Anne Murray's. She doesn't belt out tunes the way that Connie Kaldor and Heather Bishop do, although she has considerable vocal power. Rather, she holds the volume steady, and the controlled emotion gives her singing great power, as though there were a bomb of passion inside her, waiting to go off.

Tremblay not only sings, she whistles. She has developed a technique for producing the whistle with the tongue rather than the lips, and by varying the pressure she can change the pitch. "For her (the whistling) is just another instrument," Karen Shopsowitz wrote in the Canadian Composer, "one which she plays as skillfully as she plays guitar and piano.... It sounds much like a pan flute and scales a remarkable range of notes. In concert, it's hard to believe that the haunting progression of notes is coming from Tremblay, and not from some backstage flautist." Sometimes members of the audience look around, as though suspicious that some birds or even Pan himself had slipped into the auditorium. "I like the colour the whistling adds," Lucie says.

She started writing her own songs, in both French and English, when she was about seventeen. "My first songs were very naive.

When you start writing, you have to release a lot of feelings, but when you are young you don't have much life experience, so you write what you think or hope life is about." Some of her early compositions were simplistic political anthems — "more like demonstration slogans," she says. Mostly she wrote "mushy love ballads" with very simple melodies which she composed on the guitar.

Soon after leaving college, Tremblay began to perform solo in bars and nightclubs. "I made the rounds until someone gave me a job. Sometimes I just showed up with my guitar and asked to audition. Somebody would give me a booking, and then through word of mouth I got other gigs." She sang a mixture of original material, contemporary songs with thoughtful lyrical content, and popular music. She disliked the bar scene. "The smoke was hard on my throat, people got drunk and obnoxious, men made sexist remarks, people played pool while I was singing. The hockey game would be on the TV. Even though the sound was turned off, people were still glued to the screen. All of a sudden in the middle of a song there would be a shout of 'Score!'"

But the bar scene wasn't all bad. "I made a living from my music. And the club circuit was like a school for me. I learned how to build and maintain rapport with the audience, even in an unpleasant, distracting atmosphere." Eventually, disagreements about her material pushed her to stop singing in bars. "The owners expected me to play music that would make people drink, make them have a good time. After a while I realized that this wasn't working for me. I wasn't a rock and roller. I wasn't happy doing background music. My choice of songs was intentional and I wanted people to listen. I was writing more songs and I wanted to sing them. Some people were beginning to come to hear *me*, but most of the people in the club just came for a good time, so it was noisy and the people who wanted to listen couldn't hear."

Lucie quit the bar scene and began to play at coffee houses, colleges and universities. Although she was glad to get out of the clubs, her income dropped drastically and she was forced to take another job. She became a school bus driver, practicing guitar on the bus and singing with the children. "I had one group of kids that I drove home for lunch. They would run into their houses, grab their lunches and hurry back to the bus to sing with me."

In the summer of 1981 Lucie toured the Gaspésie-lower St. Lawrence region of Quebec, playing in coffee houses and cultural centres in towns like St-Jean Port Joli, Rivière-du-Loup and Rimouski. She traveled on a motorcycle which she had modified for the trip by removing the back rest and building a platform for her luggage and guitar. This was her first exposure to life outside

Montreal. "Sometimes you forget that there's more than big city life. The country was very beautiful and peaceful. Traveling on my motorcycle, I was in the *décor*, not in the little box of a car, passing through. I smelled the salt water and the hay and the manure in the fields. Sometimes at night when I was driving to the next town, I'd stop the bike, lie down in the grass beside the road and look at the stars. I'd never done that before." She discovered as well a new kind of human interaction. "In the small towns I saw people touching without sexual connotations, looking each other in the eye, really listening to one another. I was used to everyone rushing around, not trusting each other. People were very real."

Tremblay was especially impressed by St-Jean Port Joli, the home of a wood sculpture school and a centre for artisanship in the province. The gentle pace of life she found there was like a fragrant breeze, and she captured the spirit of the place in the song "St-Jean Port Joli":

> *Deux heures de l'après-midi et la mareé descend...*
> *Le soleil il perce les nuages*
> *Et avec un oeil magique, j'observe les oiseaux sauvages...*
> *St-Jean Port Joli, je t'emmène dans ma vie...*
> *Que c'est bon d'apprendre à vivre au ralenti.*
>
> *(Two o'clock in the afternoon and the tide is going out...*
> *The sun breaks through the clouds*
> *And with magic eyes I watch the wild birds...*
> *St-Jean Port Joli, I carry you on through my life...*
> *How good it is to learn to live in slow motion.)*

That trip was a turning point in Tremblay's consciousness. "It made me discover a different philosophy of life. I became receptive to the earth, to people's needs, to birds and the ocean, to different issues. It gave me a good feeling, which I've tried to keep with me ever since. When I returned to Montreal I wanted to give, to do something positive."

She translated that impulse into action by conducting theatre improvisation workshops in men's and women's prisons with an actor friend, Alain Gabriel. "I wanted to help the inmates put energy into something creative." Although Lucie had no background or training in theatre, her experience as a performer had given her a sense of drama. She and Alain gave the inmates a theme or starting point, around which they created short dramatic pieces. After a while she began to do workshops on her own, changing the focus from theatre to music. Once a week she brought in her guitar, congas, bongos, other percussion instruments and an extra guitar. Working with twelve to fifteen inmates at a time, she had them make up songs or, if they wished, she improvised music and they added words. As a member of ARCAD, a recreational and cultural association for inmates, Lucie conducted the workshops for several years.

She noticed important differences between men's and women's prisons. "The men had more and better facilities for recreation, education and culture. They had a skating rink, body building equipment, a running track, a studio where they could do sculpture and painting. The women's jail had a gym but no track, a crummy swimming pool. Their activities depended more on volunteers who came in and initiated things. There was an attitude that women were less important, that they didn't need or deserve as many chances to get recreation or learn new skills."

Tremblay says she was never afraid while working in the prisons. "The prisoners were like people we see every day, but they'd got caught. The hardest lesson for me was realizing that the prison system was there not to rehabilitate but to punish. That disturbed me because I think it's better to work for growth and change, and the system doesn't do that." The song "Laissez-moi sortir" ("Let Me Out"), about a woman convict, came out of these experiences.

> *Laissez-moi sortir, mon âme est en train de mourir*
> *Laissez-moi retrouver les sourires oubliés*
> *Je pense que j'ai assez payé.*
>
> *(Let me out, my soul is dying*
> *Let me discover those forgotten smiles*
> *I think I've paid enough.)*

Through the early '80s, Lucie continued to play the coffee house-college circuit, then began to perform at women's events and folk festivals. In 1984 she won the Singer-Songwriter Award, the Press Award and the Public Award at the 16th Annual Song Festival in Granby, Quebec—an almost unprecedented sweep of all three prizes that made front-page headlines in Quebec newspapers. She appeared at the Michigan Women's Music Festival and was the surprise star of the Canadian Women's Music and Cultural Festival in Winnipeg in 1985. That same year she was asked to perform a theme song for the Francophone Festivities in Quebec; she sang Guy Trepannier's "On recommence à vivre" ("We Start to Live Again") and recorded it as a single. She began to tour in Canada and the United States.

In 1985 Tremblay came to the attention of Olivia Records, the first women's music label in the U.S. Judy Dlugacv, president of Olivia, recalls, "A friend of mine, Irene Young, went up to Canada that summer and heard Lucie at a folk festival. She was greatly impressed and asked Lucie for some tapes, saying she wanted to show them 'to a friend who had something to do with records.' Lucie gave her some. Irene came back to California, handed me the tapes and said, 'I have your next recording artist. I'm going to bring her down her and put on a small concert and you're going to sign her.''

"Well, I was skeptical but Irene was so certain that I went along with it. Lucie came down to California and played the concert. When I heard her, I knew Irene was right. We signed her immediately." In 1986 *Lucie Blue Tremblay* was released on Olivia Records in the U.S.; it will likely be released in the fall of 1988 in Canada.

All but one of the songs on the album are original compositions. For Tremblay, songwriting is a process of expressing the emotions she feels. "I need to be moved emotionally before I can write a song. I start by feeling an emotion, and it inspires a chord, a rhythm, a musical progression. The chord makes me feel the emotion even more strongly. I nurture that emotion, go deep into it, and the words emerge from it. It can be very masochistic if the initial feeling is sadness or pain," she says, bursting into laughter. "I go from that first chord to another and then another, and there's the whole song." She carries a notepad and pen everywhere, even in her bicycle saddlebag, to jot down words and ideas; later, the emotion may direct her to retrieve those scribblings for a song. She usually works out the melody vocally, then plays it on the guitar or piano, whichever is handy. For some songs, she hears only guitar accompaniment and vocal harmonies, for others she hears complex instrumental arrangements. When traveling, she carries a portable tape deck to record melodies that come to her.

Lucie says that the "colour" of the song tells her whether to write in French or English. "Each language has different sounds and frequencies. A song might need the soft French 'r' or the harder guttural sounds of English." When she began to write songs, she wrote mostly in English: because of her schooling she was intellectually stronger in that language. After a while, however, she realized that her spoken and written French were suffering from lack of use. Determined not to lose fluency in her native language, she decided to place herself in a stronger French environment, forcing herself to think, speak, read and write more in French.

Tremblay's re-identification with French culture and language coincided with the rise of the separatist movement in Quebec — a movement she followed with interest though not with overt support. "I was never active politically in the movement. I never joined the Parti Québecois or any separatist organization. But I understood that sometimes you have to go to extremes to find a just middle ground. It takes people to stir up things and to follow through on what has been stirred up. I'm not a 'stirrer' but I'm very loyal to what I believe. I *am* French Canadian. When I sing I want people to completely understand who I am, and that includes my culture." She writes and performs half in English, half in French. "I'm very firm about the percentage of French songs I do. If I sing two French songs and the rest in English, people will get a different idea of who I am. For me, 50-50 is a healthy balance."

Besides singing half in French and half in English, Tremblay shares her French culture with her audiences, especially when she performs outside Canada. On her first tour of the United States, she brought along a Quebec flag, which she displayed onstage. She's incorporated a slide show of Quebec to go with "St-Jean Port Joli;" she asks her audiences to sing along on the line "Que c'est bon d'apprendre à vivre au ralenti" — and they do, even if they don't understand a word of French. In "Tour Song — or — O Canada," she tells how she misses Canada and longs for news of Montreal when she is away. A French Canadian girl who is taken out of her cultural milieu is the subject of "Mommy, Mommy." While she's on tour she brings a coffee bowl and espresso machine — "a bit of home," she says. "As I get older my identity as a French Canadian grows stronger, especially now that my career is more centred in the U.S."

Lucie has never encountered hostility from American audiences for singing in French. Indeed, according to Olivia Records' Judy Dlugacv, "Her efforts to bring her francophone culture to the U.S. has made a difference. She has increased people's understanding."

But at home her 50-50 policy isn't always popular. "In Canada," she says, "where the whole language question is more controversial, it always feels safer when I go into a city like Ottawa or Winnipeg, where there's a French community and people are more used to hearing French, more exposed to French culture. In some parts of Canada I feel a slight resistance from English-speaking audiences. Most people are positive but some just tolerate it. It's a delicate situation. But I don't want to talk so much about the problem, I want to do something about it. I want to make my songs in both French and English accepted all over Canada. One of my goals is to bridge that gap."

On the provincial level, she finds increasing tolerance and under-standing between English and French in Quebec. "Francophones are more accepting of English culture than before. Now, if an English-speaking person just tries to speak French, francophones will be so happy, they'll do anything to help. Before, anglophones wouldn't even try; it was always up to francophones to learn

English, and they resented that. We've made progress, and it's important to keep this progress."

From her early simplistic songwriting efforts, Lucie has matured and improved as a songwriter. "I want to be known as a writer," she says. Whichever language she's using, she tries to write like a native speaker, capturing the rhythms and phrasing of that language. "I'm not a poet but I try to write so that my songs don't sound like everybody else's. I want them to have a deep content that doesn't just say, 'Oh, I love you' or 'I can't live without you,' but something more, a new twist or a different angle. I try to do little interesting things with the words, like saying 'I'm rising in love' instead of 'I'm falling in love.'

"My vocabulary and language skills are always growing. But I want to keep my lyrics simple, keep them in touch with what I'm feeling and express myself in a way that people can understand. I don't want to get caught up in the way that I say it — I just want to say what's in my heart." This focus on simplicity is a trait she shares with Rita MacNeil.

As Tremblay's ability to use language has improved, the vision with which she writes has matured. Most of her tunes are love songs, but now her "mushy ballads" about imagined love have been replaced by realistic songs about many aspects of love. "So Lucky" is one of her early ones. "It's about falling in love, when you feel your heart will jump out of your shirt and your feet aren't on the ground."

> So lucky that I should be in love with someone like you
> No one else makes me feel the way you do
> You're making my dreams come true.

"'So Lucky,' came from a naive view of love," Tremblay says. "Some of my later songs speak with a more experienced voice" — like "Magic of Love," a song that explores the pain of letting go in a dying relationship. "'Magic of Love' describes that funny time when you're not over the relationship yet. You know it won't work but you want to hang onto the connection."

> I'm so tired of sleeping all alone
> But I'm so afraid of falling in love
> So many times I've wished that you'd come home
> But it isn't you I want, it's the magic of love.

The unraveling of a relationship is also the subject of "Nos belles annees," Lucie's French adaptation of Ferron's "Ain't Life a Brook." "When I heard Ferron's *Testimony* album, I loved that song. I did a loose translation of the words and then made a tape.

I went to the Michigan Women's Music Festival, where Ferron was singing, and left the tape with her. A little while later, she came to Montreal to play. She looked for me before her concert—I was in the audience—and asked me to perform the song with her that night. I was thrilled to join her onstage. After the show she told me she liked my version a lot and gave me permission to record it."

Lucie's rendition of the song is different from Ferron's in more than just language. When Ferron sings it, there is a cynicism, a kind of dry wit, that shields her—and us—from the pain of what she is describing. Lucie takes hold of that pain, wraps it around herself like a cloak, and then marches out into the storm of the song, holding her face up to be lashed by the wind and rain. Her voice trembles as she sings, *"On est allé au restaurant/Prendre une bièrre tout en parlant de nos belles années"* (In Ferron's words: *"Went out to dinner one more time/Had ourselves a bottle of wine and a couple of laughs")*.

"Limited Vision" is another song that explores a difficult aspect of love in its honest look at the tradeoff between long term commitment and physical attraction:

> *I gotta look good, I gotta feel good*
> *I gotta make believe I'm happy when I know that I'm feeling sad*
> *Let me tell you something, baby, I'm losing all that I had*
> *For something physical, so physical*
> *I used to think it was all right*
> *To be with someone for just one night*
> *But if it meant the end of us, I'd let the passion go by.*

Tremblay may address the pain of love, but more than most singer-songwriters, who tend to dwell on the troubling aspects, she writes about the joy of love. Smiling broadly, she say, "Being in love is positive in my life, it's a positive exchange between my lover and me. When I'm in love I grow a lot. I like the emotion itself and also the give and take of relationships. There's something precious about love that's important to capture." When she says she's *"so lucky... to be rising in love with you,"* we can't help but recall our own first intimations of romance, and relive their sweetness along with her.

Although Tremblay does not write overtly feminist songs, a sense of feminism runs through her work. She is among the first generation of Canadian singer-songwriters (along with people like Lorraine Segado, Jane Siberry and k.d. Lang) to have as models women musicians who came through the Canadian folk scene and who themselves were influenced by the women's movement— women like Ferron, Connie Kaldor, Heather Bishop and Rita

MacNeil. "The first musician I heard doing women's music was Cris Williamson. Soon after that, around 1979, I first heard the Canadian women musicians. Heather, Connie and Ferron blazed a trail for me. They were out there as Canadian women musicians long before I started, and I have followed in their footsteps. I remember the first time I saw Ferron perform at a folk festival. I felt proud and inspired. She's made a path for a lot of women singer-songwriters. So has Heather Bishop. I admire not only the strength and power of her voice but also the way she's stayed true to her values and her music."

Tremblay considers herself a feminist but says, "Ten years ago it was more 'in' to talk about feminism; now it's just a way of life. I'm not a feminist writer, I'm just a person who writes with a feminist and a human vision because of where I'm at in my life. Just by the path my words take and by the strength I give myself as I'm writing a song, you can feel it's not a victim who's writing it."

She calls her music "women's music," but points out, "The term 'women's music' was started in the United States. I listened to Heather Bishop for a long time without realizing that her music fit into some category; it wasn't until I went to the States that I came across the label. There are many definitions of women's music, just as there are many definitions of feminism. Some people define it as women playing with other women musicians to women audiences. In that sense my music isn't women's music because I have men playing on my album.

"I want to reach everyone with my music, not just women. Some people have the idea that women's music is only for women or feminists. That's not true. Somehow we've got to change that attitude. We've got to make people realize that our music doesn't exclude anybody. Maybe the answer is to get rid of the label."

Tremblay's feminism is closely related to her sense of social justice. Here, too, her growth as a songwriter shows in the transformation of her early "demonstration slogans" into more subtle political songs. Perhaps her best-known composition with a political-social theme is "Voix d'enfant," about incest, a subject that is close to her. When she read a newspaper article about a man who got his daughters pregnant in order to receive more welfare payments, she was inspired to write a song. "It's the kind of subject that must be made accessible so that someone who has experienced it and feels they're the only one, knows they're not alone. Music isn't all writing light, happy songs; it's also writing songs that have a purpose, that help people talk about painful subjects." "Voix d'enfant" uses the persona of a young girl who is assaulted by her uncle.

Je suis une enfante, j'ai honte, j'ai mal en dedans
Je suis une enfante, je me sens coupable en dedans
Il prend ma main, j'me sens pas bien... je me sens tout seule
Il vient dans mon lit, puis je ne lache pas un cri...
Je ne peux pas en parler.

(I am a child, I'm ashamed, I'm sick inside
I am a child, I feel guilty inside
He takes my hand, I don't feel well.... I feel all alone
He comes into my bed, but I don't scream...
I can't talk about it.)

"Voix d'enfant" has been chosen as the theme song for a video on incest produced by the Montreal Centre for Social Services, which will be shown on television and used to educate school students, social workers and police officers. The film explains the steps children can take to protect themselves when they speak out about incest. As well as the theme song, Lucie has composed the instrumental score for the entire video. She welcomes the recent resurgence of interest in music that champions social justice.

Most of Lucie's songs are slow, melodic ballads with soft-sounding vocals and simple instrumental lines. "My forte is ballads," she says. The melodies are pleasant and very hummable, the kind of tunes that roll around in your head for days after hearing them. She sometimes writes in other styles; a new song about teenage suicide, for instance, has a more modern, hard-edged sound. French Canadian musical influences are not evident on her first record, but she'd like to use more traditional elements such as accordion and harmonica — "French colour with a modern sound," she calls it.

Like most singer-songwriters, she is frustrated by the imposition of stylistic labels on her music. To solve the dilemma, she calls her music 'folk-pop.' At the same time, she acknowledges that labels are important in marketing. "The important thing is to be open about labels, to not expect musicians to stay in the same category forever. Maybe I could put out a new label called 'the emotional label,'" she says, waving her hands and wailing like a baby.

Lucie's sense of humour and play is well-known among her friends and fellow musicians. While she was recording her album she played catcher on a Montreal softball team. When Judy Dlugacv heard about that, she called Tremblay and said, "You can't do that! You might get hurt. What if you got hit on the hand?" Lucie assured her that everything would be all right and continued to play. Later she did get hit in a game and was knocked out — but she didn't tell Judy until after the album was recorded.

Lucie is a sincere and engaging performer. In *The Spectator*, Kathleen Wernick said, "Tremblay has a genuine warmth and is a natural comedian, which makes for a phenomenal rapport with her audience." Like Connie Kaldor, she comes alive under the spotlight. She shares humourous anecdotes, rolls her eyes and shrugs her shoulders in a self-deprecating way that communicates to the audience that she is one of them, with the same problems and jealousies and small triumphs. "The essence of her strength is how she relates to the audience," Dlugacv says.

Lucie agrees. "Performing is my favourite thing," she says, leaning forward in her seat as if to emphasize the point. "It's a big exchange. I get to live what I put out in a song and exchange that for the audience's energy. I like to touch others with the same emotion that made me write the song. In concert we are all on common ground. We are all part of the same emotion."

Her performing schedule can be exhausting: a recent tour had her doing nine concerts in ten days with six airplane rides. "By the last concert I don't have the same energy that I did for the first or second. I pray to get through the show. But then magic happens. I get on the stage, start the first song, the people put out this energy and before I know it the concert is over and I've had a great time. I've got tears in my eyes because people have been so loving. That magic is precious. It keeps me going."

Tremblay now supports herself through performances and record sales. "I feel privileged. For a long time I had to have other jobs. Now I can do what I love to do and get paid for it." She enjoys playing for any size crowd, from seventy-five people in a coffee house to 7,000 at a folk festival. At a concert in San Francisco during her fall 1987 tour, she was singing in a ninety-seat dinner-theatre when there was a power failure. There were no lights, no amplification. "I went around the room with my guitar and sang from table to table. The audience loved it and so did I. It was really nice to go back to living-room playing." As a new feature of her performances, she uses an interpreter for the hearing impaired. She describes her ideal performance as a concert in which she'd open for herself. "I'd play alone for the first set, then have a band and vocalists for the second set."

As Lucie prepared to make her first album, she wanted to produce something that would be both artistically satisfying and commercially appealing. "My priority was to have the lyrics as emotional and conscious as possible, combined with a good quality production and a popular sound like music on the radio." She persuaded Olivia Records to let her record one side in the studio and the other live, giving the album a mixture of pop and folk "colours," as she says.

Judy Dlugacv recalls, "Lucie put a tremendous amount of pressure on herself by wanting to have one whole side taped live. The San Francisco Bay area audience wasn't that familiar with her. She had to win them over. But she wanted to do it that way. She knew she worked well as a live performer. She had so much confidence in herself that we agreed to give it a try."

It worked. On the live side, which was taped at the Great American Music Hall in San Francisco, she plays solo, accompanying herself on guitar and piano, with vocal backup on one cut. The songs have a simple, clean, acoustic sound that allows her warm voice and her engaging personality to dominate.

Tremblay wanted to record the studio side in her home town, and she searched long and hard to find the right producer. "I needed someone who was good in the studio but also open to ideas and who loved my music. I gave one of my songs to different arrangers to see what they would do with it. Daniel Loyer put out the emotion I felt in the song, so I decided to have him arrange and produce the studio side." The songs were recorded at Studio Victor in Montreal on 24-track equipment using studio musicians.

Lucie has been pleased with her collaboration with Loyer. "He has come up with the arrangements and accompaniment I want. The more we work together, the more we complement each other. Sometimes we listen to a tape, and just by exchanging a look we both know what's wrong and what's right with it."

The studio side of the album is very pop-sounding, and the emotion in her voice is somewhat subdued by the smooth backup vocals, strings and synthesizer accompaniment. Tremblay acknowledges that the studio side isn't as warm. "That wasn't entirely intentional. It was a result of not having people to sing to. The audience brings out the warmth in me. When I record in the studio I have to bring in a rug, incense, candles; I have to dim the lights to try to make it intimate and warm. At the same time I have to be careful to make my delivery blend with the other instruments and fit the overall sound."

Still, she feels the degree of production on the studio side was necessary and worthwhile. "It was consciously designed for a commercial sound. I wanted to get radio play. I'd like people driving in cars to hear my music."

Her approach appears to be working. At her most recent appearance in Boston, she sold out a 1200-seat hall, more than doubling the attendance from her last visit. *Lucie Blue Tremblay* has received rave reviews and sold over 20,000 copies in the United States even before the record was released in Canada—most independently-produced albums sell half that amount. Susan Wilson, the music critic of the *Boston Globe*, named it one of the ten best records of 1986, along with such highly-acclaimed albums as Paul Simon's *Graceland*. Judy Dlugacv calls Tremblay "one of Olivia's best-selling artists."

After considerable difficulties with the U.S. immigration system, Tremblay received a work permit and moved to New Orleans in late 1987. She has since toured the east and west coasts and the southern states, including a four-city tour in April and May, 1988 with other musicians to celebrate the fifteenth anniversary of the founding of Olivia Records. She will continue performing in the States until the end of 1988 when her permit expires—then she'll reapply. Between concerts she's been writing songs and will make a second album in late 1988, again on Olivia Records.

But Canada remains home. "I miss my family and friends. I miss Montreal and the sound of French." She returns for visits and to play occasional concerts, and will tour Canada when *Lucie Blue Tremblay* is released in this country.

A mixture of idealism and pragmatism guides Tremblay's career. Ever the realist, she gives her songs up-to-date production. Ever the romantic, she refuses to sacrifice the integrity of her messages and listens to the counsel of her heart. From the blue in her hair to the emotions that compell her to write, Lucie Blue Tremblay strives to express the colours of the song.

A Woman's Pride

"Even when times are hard we need music. We need to get filled up so we can go back out there and keep fighting. Part of my job is to fill people up, to keep them charged, to keep them proud."

*H*eather Bishop was twenty-five years old in 1974. She was living in Regina, playing electric guitar and piano in an all-woman dance band called Walpurgis Night. They played country music, polkas, schottisches, waltzes, blues and rock and roll in cities and small towns all over the province. One night the lead singer quit. The band members pushed Bishop to the front and told her to sing.

"But—but—I can't sing," she protested.

She meant it. She'd been told as a child that she was tone deaf and was convinced that she could not—and should not—sing.

The band was merciless. "Sing," they commanded. Bishop opened her mouth and sang. Within weeks she'd mastered forty songs and become Walpurgis Night's new lead singer. Two years later she launched a solo career as a musician and singer, a career now entering its second decade.

Slim, wiry, athletic-looking, Heather seems to have energy coiled in her muscles even when she is still. She dresses simply—off stage, jeans and a sweater, on stage, slacks and a men's style tailored suit jacket, sleeves rolled up, a colourful scarf draped around her neck. No glitz. No hype. Honest good looks and, as Kate Clinton says, "a voice as big as Manitoba."

Heather Bishop was born in Regina in 1949 and grew up there.

From an early age she was interested in music, though neither of her parents was musical. When she was five her parents salvaged a piano from a fire for $50. She started taking lessons, continuing through the grade nine level and later putting herself through university by teaching piano. "I always felt comfortable on the piano and loved playing it," she says.

When she was thirteen Bishop saw Nina Simone on television and was moved by a kind of music she'd never heard before. "I didn't know that was blues, I didn't know what it was. I just knew that I loved it. She played and sang like nothing I'd heard before. Until then I was a little piano player, playing nice little chords and melodies. She played so powerfully, the piano seemed to shrink under her hands. And I liked what she was singing *about*—prejudice, freedom, sexuality. She opened up new ideas for me about what music was and what it could do." Bishop began listening to Simone's records, and, through them, discovered women blues singers like Billie Holiday, Bessie Smith and Big Mama Thornton. Bishop devoured the blues. "To some extent I missed out on rock and roll in the '60s and '70s because I was hooked into the blues."

She was aware, though, of the folk music revival. In high school she wanted to learn to play guitar. A blind friend of hers was a fine guitarist, so they set up a trade: he taught her guitar and she read to him. Bishop loved the fresh sound of folk music, and was inspired by the content—especially by songs of Buffy Sainte-Marie and Tom Paxton. Again and again in conversation she refers to Simone, Sainte-Marie and Paxton as people she still admires. "I respect them not only as musicians but also for their courage to talk about all aspects of their lives, including the oppressive aspects like racism. That wasn't a safe thing for them to do but they did it anyway. And there was something genuine about all of them. I felt that if I met them they would be the same people I saw on the stage."

Although Bishop has never met Simone or Paxton, she has worked with Buffy Sainte-Marie. "She's sincere and down to earth. She plays benefits on reserves without lots of publicity, even when it isn't part of a tour. She isn't a star-tripper, just an ordinary person."

While she was growing up, Heather wanted to be a veterinarian or an artist. "I loved to draw. I always had a pencil or crayon in my hand and was sketching what I saw around me or in my imagination. Recently my brother found a pastel drawing I'd done when I was about eight, of a cougar on a rock bluff. It was pretty good! I hadn't realized that I had a flair for art so young."

Bishop attended the University of Regina, where she majored in pottery and painting, and graduated in 1969 with a Bachelor of Fine Arts. Art school was difficult for her. "At the time realism was out and abstract painting was in. I was a realist. I didn't get any

support for the kind of painting I was doing. One of my professors said, 'Why are you wasting your time painting this shit?' I learned lots of technical stuff but I was stifled artistically — so much so that I didn't paint at all for a few years after graduation."

After university, Bishop worked at various jobs — waitress, secretary, layout artist, business manager for the university students union in Regina, hired farm hand, teacher of a Women in the Trades course at Red River College in Winnipeg, organizer of the Women in Trades organization, secretary to a field worker with the Métis Society of Saskatchewan, and community development officer with native groups in Saskatchewan. That last job was a catalyst: living in the north, being away from the academic environment, and working with native people had a liberating effect on her art. She was free to paint again. "I don't know what had been blocking me or how I got unblocked, but starting to paint again was like rediscovering my creative self. I learned that I have a burning creative spirit in me, and that if I don't express it, I won't survive."

Over the next few years she produced more than one hundred pictures, mostly portraits of older people. "I loved to paint men and women whose faces told the stories of their lives." Two of these paintings later appeared on the covers of her first two albums.

Ironically, though, as Heather rediscovered her artistic spirit, she realized she no longer wanted to be an artist. "I saw that art was bought and sold as an investment. I didn't want to be part of that. I wanted people to hang my pictures on the wall because they liked them, not because they thought they would go up in value." As well, she learned the difficulty of surviving as an artist. "I was selling paintings but I wasn't making enough to live on. I saw that I'd have to work at paying jobs on the side and not be able to devote myself to painting."

After leaving her job in northern Saskatchewan, she moved to Regina. A friend there had started an all-women band called Walpurgis Night, and asked her to join. Although Heather had played piano and guitar for years, she'd never performed publicly. "At first I was reluctant and scared. But everyone else in the band was really green and I figured I played as well as the rest of them. Besides, it sounded like fun. I was interested in feminism and was intrigued by the idea of an all-women band. No one else was doing anything like that."

But she had a lot to learn. The first lesson was how to blend her playing with the other musicians. And when she took over as lead singer she quickly mastered other skills — stage presence, fronting a band, and projection. "As the night wears on, the crowd gets drunker and drunker and louder and louder, so you really have to know how to belt the songs over their noise without straining your voice." She had always had confidence in her instrumental ability; now she was gaining confidence in her singing. After a year or so, she was ready to sing solo, and left the band.

Bishop was tired of city life by then and longed to live in the country. In 1975 she moved to Manitoba, where, with her friend Joan Miller and other women, she bought a 160-acre farm near Woodmore, about an hour's drive south of Winnipeg. They still live on the farm, which Heather describes as "table-top flat." The land is half poplar and scrub oak forest and half hay fields, which they rent to a neighbouring farmer. Bishop had learned carpentry from her father and had studied electrical wiring, so she became the crew boss when the women built three houses on the property.

Now that she and Joan were settled in the country, they tried to figure out how to make a living. Joan had been a government writer and researcher: skills not in demand in Woodmore. So it was decided — Heather was to become a professional musician, with Joan as her manager. "We figured all we needed was a telephone and proximity to an airport," Bishop says, smiling at their brashness.

At the time she was not yet writing her own songs. She'd met Connie Kaldor in 1974 in Moose Jaw. Both of them performed at a N.D.P. fundraiser, and Bishop was impressed by Kaldor's songwriting. She also admired the work of Saskatchewan writer Karen Howe. "I didn't feel the need to write because I had such excellent songwriters around me. I loved Connie's and Karen's songs, so when I thought of going solo, I turned to their material and, of course, to the blues."

Heather was determined to sing more than just pretty songs. "I'd been very political since university days. I'd worked to stop the war in Vietnam and help draft resisters get into Canada. I was involved in the peace movement and the struggle for native self-determination. I was a feminist and an out-lesbian. I decided from the beginning of my solo career that I'd be myself and wouldn't hide anything. I'd be like my musical heroes, Nina Simone, Buffy Sainte-Marie and Tom Paxton. I knew that if I couldn't be myself onstage, I wouldn't do a good job of faking it. But I honestly felt in my heart that it wouldn't work."

She soon had the opportunity to test her principles. Her first major concert as a solo musician was at the Regina Folk Festival in 1976, where she sang a Kaldor song "I Found a Girl," about the ostracism a woman suffered after declaring her lesbianism. An audience of eight hundred men and women gave Heather a standing ovation. "It blew my mind," she says. "I thought, 'Maybe it *will* work.' I decided to really go for it as a musician."

But it was difficult in the '70s for a solo woman musician. There were few role models, few doors open. Joni Mitchell and Buffy Sainte-Marie had gone to the United States. Rita MacNeil was writing and singing feminist songs, but mostly at women's events. Sylvia Tyson was performing solo, but was not singing political material. Marie-Lynn Hammond was just launching her solo career. Connie Kaldor and Ferron were, like Bishop, new to the folk circuit. In the U.S. Olivia Records was recording and promoting women's music, but there was no comparable company in Canada. Opportunities to perform were limited: only about 10 percent of all acts at Canadian folk festivals were solo women musicians. (That has now climbed to about 50 percent at some festivals.)

Bishop made a demo tape and, with that and her reputation from Walpurgis Night, she began to get gigs in Saskatchewan. She and Joan created a new concert circuit. "Joan would call an organization like the Saskatoon Rape Centre and ask them to sponsor a concert. Joan taught them how to produce a show — how to book a hall, how to do publicity, where to sell tickets, everything. I'd come and do the concert and then move on to the next women's centre or birth control clinic. At the beginning of my solo career, apart from folk festivals and the odd coffee house, all my gigs were ones that Joan and I encouraged these groups to put on. We built a circuit that way."

In 1979 Heather and Connie Kaldor toured the prairies with a show called "Saskatchewan Suite in Two Acts." Gradually Bishop's audiences evolved from mostly women to mixed crowds, and her venues from women's centres to concert halls and theatres. "Connie, Ferron and I were the first wave of women musicians to sing feminist material outside of the women's movement," she says.

Her first national exposure coincided with her first meeting with Sylvia Tyson, in the late '70s. "Touch the Earth," the CBC Radio show that Sylvia hosted, made a cross-Canada tour, stopping at CBC studios along the way to record local musicians. Bishop was one of those chosen in Winnipeg. This was her first radio gig, and her first studio experience, and she was nervous about singing "for a star like Sylvia Tyson." Heather arrived at the studio with her guitar and the sheet music for "Lucille," a Connie Kaldor song about a native woman who moves from the reserve to the city. The studio guitarist had trouble because Bishop's version of the song didn't conform to his music. The producer asked Heather to change her arrangement.

"I tried," she says, "but I was so nervous and so used to playing the song the other way, I just couldn't. I was really struggling. Then Sylvia came out from the glass booth and said in a calm, quiet voice, ' I think we should let her play it the way she plays it. She's doing just fine.' I thought 'Oh God, thank you.' It was such a little thing but her support meant so much." The radio exposure made Bishop's name known outside the prairies. It was also the beginning of her long-standing friendship with Tyson.

By the late '70s Bishop was thinking about making an album. She was attracted by the idea of signing with a major label. But she'd seen other musicians get tied to lengthy, binding contracts, and worse, lose artistic control of their music. Producing the record herself, though, seemed impossibly complicated. Then she met Dan Donahue, a Winnipeg guitarist who had put out his own first album. He offered to help produce and mix Bishop's record. They went into the studio—a basement facility with eight-track equipment—and recorded *Grandmother's Song*, released in 1979 on Heather's independent label, Mother of Pearl Records. Their collaboration proved so satisfactory that she's had Dan produce all her albums: *Celebration* in '81, *I Love Women Who Laugh* in '82, *A Taste of the Blues* in '87, and her two children's records, *Bellybutton* in '82 and *Purple People Eater* in '85. "Working with Dan is a blessing," she says. "He deserves total credit for how wonderful my albums sound."

Bishop's love for the blues has stayed with her through the years. Songs by her model, Nina Simone, are well-represented on her albums, from the sultry "Sugar in My Bowl" (*"I want a little sweetness down in my soul/...I want steam on my clothes"*) to the passionate "Do I Move You?" (*"When I touch you, do you quiver/From your head down, do you shiver?/...The answer better be yeah, yeah! That pleases me."*)

Heather moves from classics like "Am I Blue?" and "Cry Me a River" to contemporary blues like Randy Newman's "Guilty," in which her low-pitched voice nearly growls its desperation: *"I just can't stand myself/...Takes a whole lot of medicine, darlin', for me to pretend I'm somebody else."*

Blues and feminism seem an unlikely match. The form is often sung by all-male bands, with lyrics that are sexist, patronizing and sometimes even violent toward women. But over the years many women blues artists have expressed the strength of women. Heather Bishop searched out tunes like Ma Rainey's saucy "Prove It On Me Blues," in which the narrator's feminist sympathies contain a hint of lesbianism:

> *I went out last night with a crowd of my friends*
> *They're most of them women 'cause I don't like no men*
> *They say I do it, ain't nobody caught me*
> *Sure got to prove it on me.*

"Blues for Mama," by Nina Simone, is about wife battering—a subject kept a shameful secret back when she wrote it. *"They say you're mean and evil and don't know what to do/That's the reason that he's gone and left you black and blue."*

The progression of blues material from Bishop's first record to her last illustrates how her singing has matured. Although her deep, throaty voice has always been well suited to the form, on *Grandmother's Song* her approach lacks intensity; the treatment is too careful, too white. It sounds as though she lacks confidence in her singing or simply has not lived enough to know the blues. Only rarely does she cut loose and let her voice sizzle.

On *Celebration*, however, and especially on *A Taste of the Blues*, her delivery is less restrained. She has more vocal control; notes slide up and down the register smoothly. And there's more variation in the treatment of each song. She purrs like a simmering kettle, then blows off steam in a full-voiced passion. With each album she sounds more in command of the genre.

Bishop agrees her voice sounds restrained on the first record. "It wasn't that I was inhibited or didn't have a feel for the blues. It was really a lack of vocal training. I didn't know how to use my voice fully then." After *Grandmother's Song* was released she began taking voice lessons from Alicja Seaborn, a Winnipeg singing teacher. "I learned that my voice is an instrument and can be trained. When I started working with Alicja, I had a range of about an octave and a half. Now it's much larger. I've learned not only how to use my voice well, but how to take good care of it, which is just as important."

The proof lies in her rendition of Billie Holiday's "Tell Me More and More" on her most recent album. She sings with power and yet with subtlety, at times crooning forcefully, at others dropping her voice to a moaning whisper. She uses all the shades of texture at her command to express longing and sensuality: *"When you done told me about a million times how much you love me/And you're through—start right back in again."* The song truly casts a spell in blue.

The critics agree. The *London Free Press* said, "Bishop's vocals are deep, dusky, capable of sending shivers down your spine and making your hair stand on end." A reviewer for the *Halifax Mail-Star* wrote, "Believe me, when she hauls back and hits you with the first strong notes...the roof could cave in and nobody would move."

If the blues is the major stylistic force in Heather Bishop's music, then social justice is the primary theme. She is known as a singer who speaks out for what she believes in, both within and outside of her music. Quoted in *NeWest Review*, she said, "I'm a feminist because I'm a woman. It's from living my life that I became a feminist. It's from never having received equal pay for work of equal value. It's from seeing men get breaks that women didn't get...It's from watching friends get beaten by their husbands. It's from seeing men and women who have children not having day-care for them.''

Yet, like other women musicians, she sees herself as more than just a feminist songwriter. ''When interviewers ask me why I'm a women's performer, I say, 'I'm just writing what I see through this woman's eyes.' That's not so different from what Johnny Cash does. The label 'women's music' is overblown. When a man sings from his point of view it's not remarked on, not called 'men's music.' It's just called music. It's important to talk about feminism and women's lives and concerns, but music by women isn't really different from music by men.''

Bishop carefully selects songs by other people that reflect her feminist vision. ''Grandmother's Song,'' by Connie Kaldor, paints the portrait of a strong, independent immigrant woman who has led a hard life on the Canadian prairies. Matching the verbal picture is Heather's painting of an old woman on the cover of the album. Her face is creased with wrinkles. Her white hair is drawn back from her face, a few wisps straggling out from under a faded kerchief. Her jaw is square and firm, and her eyes stare defiantly at the viewer, *''Blow, you old wind of time / You've wrinkled my face with your blowin' /... taken away my youth without me knowin'.''* She yells her defiance at her children who want her to move to a nursing home: *''I'll stay here on my own till that wind blows me away.''*

''Celebration,'' by Karen Howe, tells of the oppression of women: *''Your spirit in cathedrals cried like the sound of a captive bird.''* Then it rises to a grand, anthemic chorus of strength and optimism:

> *Woman, your feet were made for dancing*
> *Woman, your voice was made to carry song*
> *And your heart was made for long, strong loving*
> *Your soul to carry you along.*

On a lighter note is a bluesy tune by Dory Previn, *''Did Jesus Have a Baby Sister?''*

> *Did Jesus have a baby sister? Was she bitter, was she sweet?*
> *Did she wind up in a convent, did she end up on the street,*
> *On the run, on the stage, did she dance?*
> *Did He have a sister?... Did they give her a chance?*

The mythical sister privately whispers to the mirror: *''Saviourette, saviour-person, saviour-woman,''* then gives up in disgust: *''Save your breath.''* This brilliantly sardonic song has become one of the most requested numbers in Heather's repertoire.

Heather addresses the subject of incest in Deborah Romeyn's

"Daddy's Little Girl." Her voice hits the minor notes with a dark, threatening tone.

> Everybody runs to the door when daddy gets home
> How come you're the only one that doesn't go?
> Why are you so quiet in the evenings?
> Aren't you daddy's little girl?

Ten years ago, songs about incest, child abuse and sexual abuse would not have been heard. According to Ruth Dworin, a Toronto-based music promoter, "We're hearing more and more songs about these subjects because the women's movement has struggled to bring them out into the open. Look at 'Voix d'enfant' by Lucie Blue Tremblay and Suzanne Vega's 'Luka.' The fact that 'Luka' rose so high in the charts shows that there's renewed public interest in issues of social justice."

Despite this, Heather Bishop hesitated to use "Daddy's Little Girl" on her album. "I really wondered if it was too heavy, too painful. But I sang it in concert a lot, and so many people told me how much it meant to them. I decided to record it, but to follow it with a healing song."

That song is "Spirit Healer," by Carolyn Brandy. Heather leads a chorus of women in gospel-like harmony:

> In the rape of this land many people have suffered
> Where is the spirit healer?
> ... Woman, you know you've got to change it
> Don't you know you're the spirit healer.

Bishop doesn't mean to imply that men aren't healers, but she believes "it's men's jobs to talk about their lives and their process, not mine. Men have spoken for women for so long; they need to speak about their own experience, just as we need to do about ours. I no longer need to include men in everything I say — that would be detrimental to their growth. If men feel excluded by a song like 'Spirit Healer,' they should examine why they do and maybe write their own song. Besides, women *have* been leaders in spiritual healing, so the song is appropriate."

It was a feminist issue that motivated Bishop to write her first song. "A Woman's Anger," about men's resentment of women tradespeople, was inspired by a machinist friend. "At the first shop she worked in, the men patted her on the ass, pointed her out as the token woman machinist, threatened to take her in the back and show her 'what a woman's really good for.' She was tough as nails and I thought she'd be able to take whatever they threw at her, but one night she came home from work and cried. The song was born of her anger, and also my own anger. I've had training in auto mechanics, but countless times when I've stopped to help a man whose car is broken down on the side of the road, he says, 'Don't touch my car!' 'A Woman's Anger' is about that, too."

> Buddy, what you're looking at now is a woman's anger
> Boys, what you're seeing right here is a woman's pride
> If you had half a lick of sense you'd realize
> You could learn from me
> Turn your head around, you'd be a better man
> Change who you might be.

On the front cover of Heather's fourth album, over a picture of her, are words in bold letters: I Love Women Who Laugh. She designed it that way to challenge people to buy an album that says "I Love Women." "Men should be able to relate to that—unless they hate women. Women should be able to say that they love themselves. I want all of us to get past our homophobia, whether we're gay or straight."

But I Love Women Who Laugh has had only half the sales of Bishop's other records. She shrugs, showing no sign of remorse. "It just indicates the degree of homophobia out there."

The title cut is an upbeat, jazzy number with a Latin feel. The words tumble out quickly, joyfully, like a train gathering speed. They catalogue Heather's admiration for women who love, who feel good, who are full of pride and song, and who laugh. Some people, hearing the title and the repeated phrase "I love women," assume that the song is about lesbians. Not so, says Bishop. "It's just a celebration of women. If you're not a misogynist, the song 'I Love Women Who Laugh' is for you, brother."

Bishop has always been honest about her sexual preference, both on and off stage. She insists that homosexuality causes unwarranted anxiety among heterosexuals, and often tells humourous anecdotes about predicaments she has found herself in because of her open stance. One time she and a male homosexual were guests on a radio talk show. "Today we have a practicing lesbian in the studio," the host announced, then turned to Heather and asked, "Are you sick?"

"No thank you, I'm quite well," she answered, "and I certainly don't need any practice."

She acknowledges that she has known prejudice. "I've been baited. People have been afraid of me because of my lesbianism. Early in my career I was very isolated. Men hated me and women didn't want to associate with a lesbian."

Still, she was undaunted. "I've never backed off dealing with those issues," she says, eyes flashing. Nor will she back off now. She continues to sing about women loving women, sometimes altering the lyrics of songs to give them homosexual connotations. In the tune "You Don't Own Me," she changes the line *"Don't say I can't go with other boys"* to *"Don't say I can't go without the boys."* When she sings Joan Armatrading's "Taking My Baby Uptown," about a couple encountering prejudice and hostility while walking down the street, the image is of two women strolling arm in arm. Her rendition of Gary Tigerman's gentle ragtime tune "Seduced" gives homosexual meaning to the narrator's desire to "find myself a woman who wouldn't mind seducing me."

Bishop isn't trying to sell lesbianism. It's simply a part of who she is, and she wants people to accept it as they accept her singing and her guitar playing. She sees that acceptance coming — slowly. "Women who didn't want to have anything to do with me fifteen years ago are feminists now. Men no longer feel so threatened. We've become friends and survivors together."

Closely allied to, and indeed inseparable from, Bishop's feminism is her commitment to the environment. "I live on the land because I love the land and I want to try to save her. All these issues — peace, the environment, women's rights — start rolling into one. Men in power have taken the earth and turned her into numbers and figures and abstracts in a way that we as women who give birth and are connected directly to the life process have not done. When all of us, men and women, love the female in us, we will also love the earth."

"The Northlands" is a plea to preserve the unspoiled beauty of the north and avoid the environmental destruction that has befallen more populated areas. *"Oh, the northlands, you're young and you're wild and your spirit's still free/... There's a magic that lives in your wilds, it's the spirit of all that's alive."*

"The Holocaust" speaks of the devastation of nuclear war, warning that *"radiation spreads in waves of death,"* and urging us to *"refuse the Cruise... one last chance to fend off this insanity."* Heather's voice floats menacingly above the strong rock beat and loud, new-wavish synthesizer, giving the song a hard-edged sound that suits the subject.

"Our Silence" combines her concern for the environment with her interest in native philosophy, developed while working with Métis and Indian groups. She was especially impressed by the union of spirituality and regard for the land and its creatures. "Our Silence" compares white and Indian attitudes toward the environment and, in particular, the poisoning of Mother Earth. *"Once upon a time the Great Mother held us in her hands/We were wise,"* Bishop reminds us, then hurls images of the despoilation of that natural heritage: *"Cancer is the seed waiting still...concrete and pavement...rivers run grey with waste."* The chorus, sung in moaning repetition against ocean sound effects, parallels the moaning death sighs of the earth:

> *It's our silence, silence, silence that's killing us*
> *We turn our backs while she dies*
> *Turn our backs and we die.*

About the environment, Bishop is serious-minded and direct. About love, she's light-hearted...and direct. Among contemporary Canadian musicians she is known for expressing unabashed sexuality. In "Please Me" she throws out an erotic challenge: *"How dare, how dare you stand there/Wearing all of your beauty/...Make my body sigh, drive me wild/...If you're gonna tease me, you know you ought to please me."*

Somewhat less steamy are two ballads, "Waltz Me Around" and "Yukon Rain." The "Waltz" is a slow, dreamy declaration of love's first blush: *"Waltz me around to the beat of your heart/Keeps time with mine/Can this be the start of a dance we might have many nights?"* In "Yukon Rain," northern images describe the sudden sweet pain of love: *"Like the Yukon rain you came so unexpected/...Before the leaves could turn and fall, you were on your way/...Like the northern sun that never sets, you've never left my heart."* Heather pronounces this the favourite song she's written. "I wouldn't change anything," she says. "It's perfect as it sits."

Although using some Canadian references, Bishop includes them less often than writers like Kaldor, Hammond or Nancy White. "My songs don't discuss Canadian geography or history, but I am a Canadian nationalist." She's proud of her country and what it stands for. "In Canada we have a liberal social tradition. Our politics are generally left of centre. Conservative governments may come and go, but we still have medicare. In the U.S. politics are more polarized. It's still illegal in many states to engage in homosexual acts." She's also noticed cultural differences. "Canadians are more reserved than Americans. Canadian musicians take their space onstage in a very polite way, Americans in a bigger, more aggressive way."

She's not just Canadian. She's a daughter of the prairies. "I'm a regionalist. My roots in the prairies are precious to me. Prairie people are my people." This comes through in songs like "Came for Free," about rural people's sense of neighbourliness. And her musical styles reflect her prairie ties even more than her lyrics. Ever since her days with Walpurgis Night, she's played the waltzes and polkas so beloved by her neighbours.

For Heather Bishop, songwriting usually begins with words. Phrases relating to a certain idea pop into her mind, she writes them out, and then adds music. This method has its pitfalls: "I'm verbose," she says with a rueful smile. "I get carried away with words and put too much in the song. I'm working on simplifying my songs, writing closer to the bone." She used to compose almost entirely on the piano, but because she's on the road so much she almost exclusively composes on the guitar.

She's critical of her songwriting. "I've written a few really good songs but I'm not a poet like Ferron or a wit like Connie Kaldor. I'm more a meat and potatoes writer. I'm not prolific. I'm a slow writer. Often when the Muse comes I don't stop to listen to her. I'll be out shingling my roof or something and I'll get an idea for a song, but I won't put down the hammer to work it out because I want to finish the job. I need to try to follow the Muse whenever and wherever she strikes."

Bishop has been criticized for her tendency to write heavy-handed lyrics, especially in songs with political and environmental themes. The stridency of the words sometimes clouds the heartfelt intent behind them, as in the lines *"In the end it all comes down to the big boys/Playing their deadly games with their much-more-deadly toys"* in "The Holocaust," and *"Maria up and quit the street life/She helps her sisters fight the white man's jail"* in "Keeping On."

Bishop acknowledges this tendency. "Writing issue-oriented songs without being preachy is very hard. Partly that's the nature of political music: it's difficult to be poetic with words like 'nuclear energy.' But partly it's a matter of skill. I admire Ferron and Kaldor for being able to sneak their messages into you — you're not aware of it because it's so subtle. That's the craft I'm trying to improve." She doesn't think she'll ever be well-known as a songwriter and predicts that future albums will contain about twenty-five percent original material. Still, she considers herself a good interpreter of other people's songs. "My ego is not invested in my own work, but I do have something to say. I think my perspective is valuable."

Bishop is one of only a few contemporary Canadian musicians who perform regularly for both adults and children. "Working with kids is almost the most important thing I do," she says. She sets aside two months a year for children's performances, travelling to remote northern communities under the Manitoba Artists in the Schools program. Because of her frequent appearances at major international children's festivals all over North America, she is as well known by children as by their parents. A great believer in audience participation, she gets the kids shouting, clapping, stomping, and sometimes storming the stage to act like chickens doing the "chicken reel" and cows doing the "cow-cow boogie" in "The Barn Dance."

Her two children's albums, *Bellybutton* and *Purple People Eater*, are mixtures of original material, classics like "Ghost Riders in the Sky" and "Somewhere Over the Rainbow," and tunes by Connie Kaldor (who sings backup on both records). Among Bishop's own compositions are "Sugar Blues," a swinging blues number about the awful crash that follows a sugar binge, and "Oh No Bo," about the adventures of her dog, Bo, and her female companion, Moxie. After each episode — when Bo, for example, pees on the Vancouver seawall in front of a police officer — Heather and chorus chant, *"Oh no Bo!"*

Her signature tune, though, at least among the younger set, is Kaldor's "Bellybutton." *"Oh, my bellybutton, I love you,"* Bishop croons. She has sung this song to so many children in so many places that now, wherever she goes, kids spot her and shout, "It's the bellybutton lady!"

Bishop has received great acclaim as a children's singer. A review of *Bellybutton* said, "The songs are performed with energy and good cheer, but the album doesn't have a single second's sappiness on it." *Purple People Eater* was awarded an Honorable Mention by the National Association of Independent Record Distributors in the United States.

Whether performing for children or adults, Heather brings tremendous energy and sincerity to her shows. Like her musical models, she presents herself exactly as she is, relying on her powerful voice and heartfelt delivery to reach audiences. Onstage she taps her feet, gestures, walks around, sways, closes her eyes, leans into the mike stand, laughs. She mixes impassioned singing with humourous anecdotes, treating the audience as a friend whom she respects and with whom she wants to share some funny or even embarrassing moments. Trevor Carolan, writing in *Canadian Composer*, said, "...there is something approximating a traditional prairie populism in her...style of performance. In concert, she delivers from a deeply rooted sense of community with her audience; one senses a genuine affection, a solidarity between audience and performer."

But performing didn't come naturally to her. "I'm a shy person. Because I had worked with a band first, I didn't feel comfortable onstage when I went solo — it felt strange to take all that space. I've gradually learned to feel comfortable with it." She credits her work for children with helping her become a good performer. "Kids are honest," she says with a grin. "If they're bored, they let you know it, and if they like the show they let you know. You have to be right there every minute. You have to put out a lot to hold their attention and energy. I learned those lessons with children and applied them to my adult performances."

Although she played solo for many years, Bishop has recently been performing with one or more side players, usually a bassist or keyboardist. She generally chooses musicians who've had less exposure: they've included Lauri Conger (who went on to join Parachute Club), Tracy Riley and Kris Purdy (both of whom launched solo careers), Marilyn Lerner (who has also backed up Marie-Lynn Hammond and is known as a fine studio musician) and Sherry Shute (a rock guitarist who is Bishop's current accompanist). "Playing with others helps ease the strangeness of being onstage," Bishop says. "It's more enjoyable, too, having someone to work with. And the audience has fun seeing the dynamics between the performers."

Bishop is a veteran of Canadian folk festivals, which operate differently from the system in the U.S. There, a women's music circuit has developed separately from the mainstream folk music scene, and feminist singer-songwriters like Cris Williamson and Meg Christian have played at all-women festivals and events through most of their careers. Since Canada's smaller population couldn't support both a mainstream and a women's music system, the folk festivals have always been integrated. "Canadian independent musicians have had to make it in general folk festivals, playing to mixed audiences," says Bishop. "We've had to be really good at what we did. I'm glad of that. It's made me a better musician. Canadian audiences are tough; because they're mixed, there's a greater range of expectations. But they also tend to look down on their own and elevate American performers to star status. There's an attitude of, 'You're Canadian so you can't be good.' It's harder to excite your home audience."

If the Canadian system has proved a good training ground for its own singer-songwriters, it's also served as a model for American performers. "American women musicians coming up here have had the chance to play to more than just the converted," says Bishop, "and men musicians have had to play alongside political, feminist musicians. This has affected their music and their outlook. A lot of Americans who have performed up here want to make their own system more integrated. They're using Canada as a model."

Despite Canada's less segregated music scene, Bishop, as a political, feminist, lesbian musician, has often struggled to reach beyond a narrow audience of like-minded women. "By being an out-lesbian I knew what kind of parameters I was putting around my career. There's a fairly fixed market in Canada of people who are open-minded enough to look past the issue of who's loving who and just enjoy the music. It's slowly growing but it's still small." Has she ever regretted her outspokenness, given that it has somewhat stymied her career? She grins. "Never. The artists I admire are all political. They had the courage to be honest and direct, to be themselves. This gave them longevity because they stayed true to their convictions and were never chasing the elusive popular cause. I emulate that."

In total Bishop's six albums have sold over 50,000 copies in Canada—a trifling figure for a star but, as she puts it, "a phenomenal amount of sales for a politically vocal, independent musician." And her career has been taking off recently. She was profiled on the CBC Radio programs "The Entertainers" and "Dayshift," received a Juno nomination in 1987 for Most Promising Female Vocalist, and has released a single containing two songs from *A Taste of the Blues*. For the first time, she leased an album (*A Taste of the Blues*) to an American company, Icebergg Records, to manufacture, distribute and promote in the States. She doesn't take this new recognition for granted. "It's just short of a miracle that I can make a living in music. I'm totally grateful."

In recent months Bishop has toured extensively in the U.S. For her first American concert swing in 1986, she opened for people like Kate Clinton and Holly Near, but in 1987-88 she toured with her own show. In order to gain exposure in the vast American market that is still largely unfamiliar with her music, she plans to focus her concerts there for the next few years.

But Canada will always be her home. "I realize how much I love this country when I'm away. I miss the house that my friends and I built, and the prairie sky. I miss throwing sticks to Bo and smelling the earth. I need to come back to the peace and quiet of Woodmore after being in cities and airports and on the road."

Heather Bishop is a link in a chain of feminist singer-songwriters, connecting earlier musicians like Nina Simone and Buffy Sainte-Marie who served as role models for her, to younger musicians like Tracy Riley and Lucie Blue Tremblay. "The second wave of women singer-songwriters will be more integrated into the mainstream because of the work that Connie, Ferron, Marie-Lynn and I did to open doors. They will have greater opportunities because we did our job."

Men are also a link in the chain. "Because of the impact of women's music on the industry, sensitive, humanist men singer-songwriters who used to be ignored are getting listened to now— men like Roy Forbes and Charlie Murphy. Men are going through change and growth. I think we'll see a leap among men singer-songwriters like we did among women singer-songwriters in the '70s."

The two things that motivate Heather Bishop to write and sing are her love of music and her political commitment. In *Canadian*

Composer, she is quoted as saying, "On one hand, I have to be an entertainer—people don't come to be lectured; yet on the other, there are so many things that need talking about. And music seems a very good way to present them." She adds, "Music can be a force for political change. I can be a catalyst by sparking an idea or challenging a bias. Music is a political survival thing, a sustenance thing. Even when times are hard we need music. We need to get filled up so we can go back out there and keep fighting. Part of my job is to fill people up, to keep them charged, to keep them proud."

This credo is exemplified in her song "If You Love Freedom." The verses portray the struggles of blacks in South Africa, the oppressed in El Salvador, and native Indians in Canada.

> *If you love freedom, say it now*
> *Let your voice ring out through the crowd*
> *Liberty comes but liberty goes*
> *To fight for her once is to never let go.*

From the Heart

"You reach out and you fly
There isn't anything you can't do."

1950. A little girl sits on her parents' bed in an old house in Big Pond, Nova Scotia. Hugging her knees, she listens to the voice of Loretta Lynn coming from the radio on the wooden dresser and imagines that someday she too will be a singer. She slips off the bed and goes to the parlour. Climbing onto the piano stool, she opens a tattered Stephen Foster songbook. So many times she has heard her sister play these beautiful melodies. Now she wants to try. Eyebrows furrowed in concentration, she picks out "Oh Susannah," humming as her fingers press the keys.

*A*s a child, Rita MacNeil loved to sing. As a young woman she sang in bars at night, while working in a department store during the day. Now she regularly sells out venues like Vancouver's Orpheum Theatre. Three singles from her latest album, *Flying On Your Own*, released in 1986, have had airplay on top-40 radio from coast to coast. In 1987 she received a Juno award for Most Promising Female Vocalist. Most promising female vocalist? — after sixteen years in the business? Well, never mind. Rita MacNeil has always known how to work and wait and work some more. She never stopped believing in herself, and if the industry has only just discovered her, that's their loss. And if the recognition and awards make her life a little easier, she'll accept them gratefully and keep on singing.

Rita MacNeil has a voice that cuts through appearances, right to the soul of the song, to the soul of everyone listening. Her vocal chords seem to bypass her lungs and pick up vibrations directly from her heart.

Heart: one can't avoid the word when discussing Rita MacNeil's singing. Her friend and former band member Joella Foulds says, "She puts out so much, it's like she's spreading herself out in front of the world." Listeners sense that, and can't help but feel a strong connection with her and her music.

MacNeil's speech gives her away as a Cape Bretoner of Scottish origin. Phrases rise and fall in pitch like whitecaps on the water; listening to her talk, you feel as though you are being rocked in a gently swaying rowboat. Her speaking voice is so quiet it borders on a whisper — then, when she opens her mouth to sing, you are not prepared for the powerful tones that come out. Her voice, a soprano-contralto with a strong vibrato, is full of the aching sweetness of Patsy Kline. k.d. Lang, who covers many of Kline's songs, also sings with that heartbroken sound, but with more vocal modulation, more of a bluesy, raspy shading, more twang and dramatic affectation. But MacNeil's voice is sweeter, clearer and higher. In *NOW*, Michael Hollett called it "a less stylized, richer version of Sylvia Tyson's vibrato." Rita's voice has no guile, none of the mellowness or refinement of a singer like Anne Murray. It sounds dramatic — but not because she is acting a part. Instead, she lives each song as she sings it, and that honesty creates an emotional atmosphere as dense as fog and as warm as sunlight.

Critics search for superlatives to describe her voice. Denny Boyd, writing in the *Vancouver Sun*, said that it "has the ring of Waterford crystal," and in the same paper Douglas Todd wrote, "On ballads, it ebbs and flows in great slow rhythms, like the tides of the Bay of Fundy." Stephen Pederson of the *Chronicle-Herald/Mail-Star* called her "a singer who can belt a note over the left-field fence and follow it with a phrase as soft as a caress."

"People want to hear what I have to say because it means something to me and because of the way I deliver it," MacNeil says. "It's heartfelt and real." Heartfelt because it *is* real. She doesn't just imagine being lonely, poor, lovelorn or homesick. She has lived through all of these and sings with the surety of experience.

Yet her childhood was normal and happy. Born in the village of Big Pond (population seventy-five) in 1944, she was a middle child in a brood of eight brothers and sisters. Her father, a carpenter, built and owned a general store in the town. She commemorates the beauty of his craft and his pride in his work in the song "Old Man." As she describes the buildings he has made, her voice is full of love

but also anger at the fact that he never received recognition.

> *They hold up well and they stand up strong*
> *And to think, by God, you did it all*
> *With these tired old hands that are now holding on*
> *To what's left of your life.*

"When he heard that song, he cried," she says. "He was very proud of me. Whenever I came home from a tour or a concert, he came over to see how it went." Her father died in the mid-'80s.

Rita describes her mother, who stayed home to raise her large family, as "an ordinary woman but a strong person." One of her great regrets is that her mother died without ever seeing her perform. She celebrates her beauty, both inner and outer, and her strength of character in the slow, waltz-time balled "Rene."

> *Rene wore a dress of white, white was its colour*
> *...and the life she led and the dreams she had*
> *were like so many another.*
> *Rene, in your dress of white, it soon may change its colour.*

As in many Cape Breton homes, music was important to the MacNeils, although the family didn't sing or play instruments together. "Music was a personal experience," Rita recalls. "We listened to music and sang by ourselves. Our main form of entertainment was the radio." As well, they gathered at the homes of their neighbours to listen to fiddle playing and sing traditional Maritime tunes. Her oldest sister played the piano, and Rita loved to sit in the parlour and listen. As a child she taught herself to play the piano, but she never took formal lessons and eventually lost her skills. She now plays no instruments and cannot read music. "I sometimes feel inadequate about that. But I have a strong sense of music. I can hear melodies and instrumental parts even though I don't know how to write down or play what I hear."

From an early age, Rita loved to sing but was too shy to sing for anyone. Although she fantasized about being a singer, she didn't expect her fantasy to come true. She listened to everything from country music to Hawaiian, rock and roll to opera, blues to Celtic, and sang them all—mostly to herself. Ironically, the most popular music of the early '60s, folk music, passed her by. In 1961, at seventeen, she moved to Toronto and began to work at Eaton's. She married soon after. A daughter was born in 1966, a son in 1970. Marriage, work and parenthood left little time for music.

Still, she yearned to sing. Despite her shyness, despite her lack of musical training, something deep within her needed to make music — and not just for herself. She knew she had a good voice and was able to communicate what she felt when she sang for others. But she had no conception of herself as a performer, just a mission to sing. How did she overcome her shyness? Where did she find the courage to audition? Even now, she doesn't know. Brookes Diamond, her present manager, says, "I think her belief in herself and her love of music kept her going." She worked up a repertoire of traditional folk songs and set out to find a place to sing.

> *1967. Rita is walking in downtown Toronto. A flashing neon sign beckons her. She goes into a nightclub and auditions for the manager in a dingy back room.*
> *"Sorry," he says. "We don't go in much for solo singers. People like to hear a band, rock and roll, dance music."*
> *She tries a pub.*
> *"No original material? Sorry."*
> *At the third club, the owner listens to her sing a couple of songs. "Nice voice," he says.*
> *She smiles, begins to hope.*
> *He looks her over. "Take my advice," he says. "If you want to get work in the music industry, it would be very beneficial if you showed some cleavage."*
> *Rita stands there, stunned. Then she turns and walks out.*

In the late '60s, MacNeil began to attend a women's support group in Toronto. There she met women who had experienced the same injustices she had: sexual stereotyping, unfair wages, treatment as second-class citizens. Rita underwent a political awakening. She began to understand the system and the ways it oppresses women. She began to see alternatives. Perhaps more important, in the supportive atmosphere of the women's group she found the courage to say what she felt about social issues and her own life. "The women helped me find out who I really was. I realized that what I wanted to do — what I *had* to do — was to write my feelings. It was an extension of something within me that needed to happen." Without knowing how it should be done, she began to write songs.

MacNeil's main source of inspiration, then as well as now, was her own feelings and experiences. "When I'm lost for an idea I go inside myself," she says. "It works every time." When composing, she hears words set in a melody in her head. "The melodies are very clear and strong. The words usually come fairly easily, as if they're on a string." A musician friend once suggested to her that perhaps her inability to play an instrument or read music was a blessing, that musical knowledge might hinder her spontaneous approach to writing songs. Rita shrugs and grins. "Who knows? It might be true." Of course, songwriting isn't always easy. "Sometimes I think, 'That's the last damn song I'll ever write. There's nothing left to draw on.' But then I find more inspiration.''

Her early songwriting days marked the beginning of a lonely, inward-looking phase, paradoxically during one of the most fertile periods in Canadian and American music. The early '70s abounded with gifted singer-songwriters such as Ian and Sylvia, Joni Mitchell, Gordon Lightfoot, Bob Dylan, Joan Baez and Neil Young. Folk and rock were criss-crossing in the music of people like James Taylor and The Band. But although MacNeil never stopped listening to music, she was out of touch with the contemporary music scene. She sang *a capella* and so had no contact with other musicians. And songwriting, for her, was a process of looking within. ''I wasn't aware of much other music because I was caught in the turmoil of discovering myself. I was trying to find my own voice.''

1971. The Health Collective Chairperson finishes her presentation to the Toronto women's group. "That's about it," she says. "Any new business?"

No one answers. "OK then — "

"I, uh — I have something," MacNeil says quietly.

"What is it, Rita?"

"It's, uh — a song. I wrote a song."

"A song? Let's hear it!"

Blushing, Rita stands. "It's just a little thing I wrote."

MacNeil smiles, clears her throat. She starts to sway from side to side, tapping her hand against her thigh in rhythm. Looking straight ahead, over the heads of her listeners, she begins in a clear contralto.

> *To be born a woman, you quickly learn*
> *Your body will be their first concern.*

Smiles cross some of the women's faces. Rita keeps swaying, beating the rhythm. Her voice grows louder.

> *The media, they've done so fine*
> *Exploited our bodies and buried our minds*
> *Follow their line and you're sure to be*
> *Another brainwashed member of society.*

When she finishes, there are whoops of delight. "Right on!"

"You said it, Rita!"

"More, more!"

MacNeil's shy smile turns into a grin. "That's my first song."

"Well, it sure won't be your last."

Rita grins harder. "You liked it."

"Liked it!" One of the women puts her arm around MacNeil's shoulders. "Rita — keep writing."

In the early '70s, MacNeil's marriage began to falter. (She and her husband separated in 1977.) At the same time, she was struggling to express her feelings about herself as a woman. She was still very close with her family in Cape Breton, but they were a thousand miles away. The women's group became her support system. As well as encouraging her to write, they gave her opportunities to perform at women's rallies and conventions. She worked at her job, raised her children and wrote whenever she had the chance.

By 1975 she had enough songs to make a record. She found a producer and went into a Toronto studio. As she played no instruments, she simply sang the songs to him. He came up with the arrangements and taught them to the studio musicians. "That first production terrified me," she says. "Some of the arrangements weren't quite how I perceived the songs, but I was too inhibited to ask for any changes. And I didn't know what to ask for anyway — how to get the musicians to play what I heard in my head. Luckily they stayed pretty true to what I sang for them." *Born A Woman* was released on the Boot Records label in 1975. Gary Cristall, director of the Vancouver Folk Music Festival, calls it "the first feminist album in Canada."

Most of the songs on *Born A Woman* are about women's struggles for justice, equality and freedom from sexual stereotypes — issues that Rita as a woman, wife, mother and working person faced in her own life. Although feminism was a prominent social issue in the early '70s, there was as yet little music with that theme. Olivia Records was founded in 1973, and artists like Cris Williamson and Holly Near were beginning to record feminist-oriented music, but their work was still largely unknown in Canada. In this country Sylvia Tyson, who was still part of Ian and Sylvia, had written a few feminist songs. But Rita's education in feminism came from her women's support group and the lessons of her own life. When she started writing, women's culture was only beginning to emerge in North America. Without realizing it, she was helping to create its musical component. If *Born A Woman* was a first flickering candle lighting the path of feminist music, the way is now illumined by torches carried by all the women in this book, as well as many others.

The album has an angry tone — not a shrill fury, but the recognition of injustice and the refusal to accept it any longer. Many of the lyrics are simplistic and propagandistic, filled with the righteous anger typical of political anthems. But *Born A Woman* also expresses joy and strength in its celebration of womanhood and its spirit of political change.

"War of Conditioning," a rock and roll tune, describes how society molds boys and girls into stereotyped roles: *"When she was a baby girl they gave her a doll/And they gave him a motor car and a tiny*

143

soldier boy." Then the girl is given a home and a rocking chair, while the boy receives a gun and finally a walking cane. In old age they both *"mourn for a freedom that they'd never known."*

"Angus Anthony's Store," an old-English-style ballad, has a fast, rolling guitar refrain set to a marching drum beat. MacNeil equates the powerlessness of women with that of native people and suggests that aggression conditioned in boys leads to violence and wars. She recalls childhood games:

> *The girls played the Indians for we had believed*
> *They were the mindless, inferior breed*
> *And the boys shot us down, one, two and three*
> *As they danced around in their victory.*

But this victory poses a danger to the conquerors as well as to the conquered: *"How does it feel when you're holding the power?/God help you when the gun backfires."*

In "John and Mary," people discover the truth about oppression and injustice and rise up to reform society. *"For every rebel standing there'll be one hundred more,"* Rita warns. The recurring line *"We'll all be the people we were warned about"* echoes the popular Yippie chant of the time, *"We're the people our parents warned us against."* The hint of social revolution calls to mind Dylan's "The Times They Are A'Changin'," though MacNeil's song is a more urgent call to action.

Similarly, "Angry People in the Streets" prophesies a revolution: *"One day two, the next day four/Tomorrow there'll be a thousand more/Angry people in the streets."* This message is delivered in a rollicking style that might be called electric country stomp, akin to Creedence Clearwater Revival.

Born A Woman is not entirely political. "Brown Grass," about memories and perceptions of home, foreshadows MacNeil's next record, *Part of the Mystery*.

> *I've only circled back to find many changes made by time*
> *And many changes in my mind*
> *I was looking for a place called home.*

Born A Woman was Rita MacNeil's only album with a predominantly feminist focus. "Feminist interests still concern me," she says. "Being a feminist has helped me deal with my children better and has taught me a lot about myself. But now it's more of an inner thing. I'm not out with placards anymore. Today my feminism is in living my life. It comes into my music in more subtle ways. I'm not a feminist songwriter. My music goes beyond that. It doesn't fit into any one category."

Still, she believes that there is such a thing as women's culture. "Women's culture means a woman's point of view. It's a warm, wonderful feeling that you get in the presence of women—a feeling of sharing, caring, being strong, expressing emotions. Women's music comes from a different point of view than music written by men because a person's experiences as a woman are different. It's a celebration of the lives of women."

Born A Woman was well-received within the women's movement and in folk circles. MacNeil began to perform more, singing at women's events, bars and folk festivals. This was a period that she calls "my dark time," full of loneliness and, no doubt, uncertainty about her future as a singer-songwriter. But the more she performed, the more she came into contact with other musicians. After a while she began to look outward, to see what was happening in music. She discovered people like Bruce Cockburn, Stringband, Joan Armatrading and Joe Cocker. All of them wrote in a way that was true to their own voices. They sang from the heart—and they had commercial and artistic succes. "If they can do it, so can I," she thought. She kept writing.

Back in Nova Scotia, people were beginning to hear about Rita MacNeil. Muriel Duckworth, the host of a public affairs program on television, used "Born A Woman" as the theme song for her show. She showed the album to her friend Joella Foulds, a singer and guitarist. Joella was a member of a Cape Breton women's group. When MacNeil came home for a visit in the summer of 1978, the women's group invited her to sing. Joella, who was one of the few people in Cape Breton familiar with Rita's songs, backed her on guitar.

MacNeil was both nervous and excited to sing for her fellow Cape Bretoners. "I was scared to sing for my own people, and I still am—just because it's the home-town crowd." But the concert was a great success. Not only did her music move the audience, but their response moved her. "I felt something very close and special singing to them"—something she hadn't felt in Toronto.

After her holidays MacNeil returned to Ontario and her job. But change was building within her. The following year she moved back to Cape Breton for good. "That was where I wanted to be. What was on the other side wasn't for me anymore. In spirit I never left anyway." Returning to Big Pond gave her an enormous emotional and spiritual boost. In her beloved countryside, reunited with her family, friends and neighbours, she achieved an inner peace that had eluded her in the city.

Rita began to perform around Cape Breton, and then throughout Nova Scotia and the Maritimes. For the first time she had accompaniment: Joella Foulds on vocals and guitar. "Rita would sing her songs to me," Foulds recalls, "and I'd figure out the chords. Her music isn't complicated, so it was usually easy to come up with an arrangement."

Over time, other musicians joined the group, and before long MacNeil had a band. At first they played mostly at women's events, gradually expanding to pubs, college campuses and folk festivals — wherever there was an audience. All this touring required a lot of time away from home. "Rita's kids were still small," Joella says. "She usually left them with her sister. She was always worrying about them and phoning them. It was hard for her to be away from them so much."

But when she was home, she was happy. The move to Cape Breton filled Rita with creative energy, and she entered an intense songwriting phase. By 1980 she had enough songs for another album. Keyboardist and producer Ralph Dillon was hired and *Part of the Mystery* was released on her own Big Pond Publishing and Production label.

Not surprisingly, the central theme of *Part of the Mystery* is home. As Rita puts it, it's about "rediscovering your roots, being excited about it, seeing things as if for the first time, and feeling great love for your past and your family." The tone is less political, more personal and contented than on *Born A Woman*, though the voice is still a questioning one. Lyrics are more poetic and abstract, demonstrating MacNeil's growth as a writer. And her singing has matured. The melodies are simple and very hummable, somewhat influenced by traditional folk and country styles, but the instrumentation is more complex than on *Born A Woman*.

Although "My Island Too" is the album's last song, it could easily have been the first. It shows MacNeil as the prodigal daughter, begging for permission to return home:

> I left you for profit and high adventure
> I came to a city I never knew
> The bright lights of my life have stolen me from you
> Can this be my island too?

Here her homecoming sounds tentative, but in "Black Rocks" she is more self-assured, more secure in the knowledge that she belongs there. With a Scottish lilt at each line end, she tells how Cape Breton's beauty uplifts her weary spirit:

> Can you imagine, to overcome sadness
> A trip to the black rocks is all that it takes?
> The waves will wash o'er me and the black rock will hold me
> And keep me from drifting away.

Although Nova Scotia is a frequent source of inspiration, MacNeil downplays her Canadianism. "I don't think being Canadian comes into my music. Music to me is music." Yet among Canadian women singer-songwriters, no other identifies so strongly with her home. For her, home means not only place but also family and community: roots. Accepting those roots and fitting into one's community are the source of fulfillment.

But not all the *Mystery* songs express fulfillment. In "Get Out of Here" Rita explores the idea of admitting your mistakes and going on with your life. This waltz-time country rocker is addressed to someone (herself?) who's been "taking a snooze in a river of booze."

> *When I get to drinking, I get to thinking*
> *On all the things I might have been*
> *But the could haves and the should haves*
> *All wrapped up in would haves*
> *If only for drinking this beer*

Similarly, "Remember the Good Times" is about forgiving yourself for past failings *("What I've done can't be undone/I've made mistakes one by one")* and grabbing happiness when it comes along. The theme of picking yourself up off the floor and carrying on is one that recurs throughout her work.

On *Born A Woman* MacNeil expressed a feminist viewpoint. In the title track of *Part of the Mystery* she expands that vision and writes from a universal standpoint. Concern for women's rights has given way to questions about the meaning of life:

> *Do you ever feel like a wick in a candle*
> *Part of the question and part of the answer*
> *Part of a mystery far greater than me or you?*

Part of the Mystery did better commercially than *Born A Woman*, but it hardly made Rita a star. Royalties from the two albums were certainly not adequate to support her and her children, yet once she left Toronto she didn't work at any outside jobs. Although she performed regularly, her income was quite low. "Rita never had any money," Foulds recalls. "She lived very simply. She never complained, but when she did concerts she had nothing to wear. Usually her sister made her dresses. She bought a house in Big Pond but never knew if she'd be able to keep up her payments. In 1985, the last year I was in her band, I did her income tax for her. I couldn't believe she could live on so little with two kids."

How did she do it? Once again, "faith in herself and her music" seems the only answer. That, and support from people who believed in her — her family, her friends, Joella Foulds, the other members of her band. And Ralph Dillon. For the first few years after Rita's return to Cape Breton, Joella arranged the songs, booked the concerts and negotiated the fees. After Ralph Dillon produced *Part of the Mystery*, he joined MacNeil's band as the keyboard player and became the leader, assuming responsibility for both musical and business arrangements. He's been with her since 1980; their relationship is a demonstration of loyalty on both sides. "Ralph is very tuned in to Rita," Foulds says. "They have a warm, close relationship. He's done so much to develop her career. He's been the silent power behind her. Several times he took reduced fees so she could pay the other musicians and have enough for herself and her kids."

MacNeil's present manager, Brookes Diamond, agrees. "Ralph is the guy who stuck with Rita when times were tough. She has a very close affinity with him."

1980. Rita is singing at a pub in Sydney to an audience of mostly miners and their wives. The room resounds with the clink of glasses, the hum of laughter and conversation. MacNeil nods to the band, then begins to sway as they play a slow introduction. She sings in an almost hushed voice.

It's a working man I am, and I've been down underground.

The room grows quiet. Heads turn toward the stage. Talking fades. They've never heard this song before.

And I swear to God if I ever see the sun.

Beer steins are put down. No one speaks. Rita sings louder.

Or for any length of time, I can hold it in my mind
I never again will go down underground.

A few of the men stand up. Then more and more, until by the third verse everyone is standing. The miners raise their fists and punch the air. They bellow in a low-pitched ragged chorus.

It's a working man I am, and I've been down underground.

By 1982 MacNeil had a new batch of songs. Marcandrew Cardiff of CBC Halifax had recorded "Working Man" at the Sydney pub a few years before. When he heard her new songs, he was impressed. He brought Rita and her band into the CBC studio, recorded some of the new songs and sent tapes to Capitol Records, A&M and other major labels. "They all rejected the songs," he says, shaking his head. "Said she'd never amount to anything."

He didn't give up. Following MacNeil's successful tour of Nova Scotia in 1982 he talked the CBC into financing her third album. *I'm Not What I Seem* was released in late 1983 on World Records for University College of Cape Breton.

Like its predecessors, *I'm Not What I Seem* has a unifying theme: triumphing over adversity. The first step, MacNeil seems to say, is to pick ourselves up from whatever nadir we have descended to and get on with our lives. In other words, we must accept our humanity, with all its potential for darkness and light.

"Strung Out and Crazy," which Rita wrote for a friend, is a plea for friendship and love from someone who has hit bottom with a crash. *"Hold on to me—oh God, I'm swaying.../I'm half over, half under, on top of it all"* — on top of a heap of trouble.

A standard blues number, "90% Stoned and 10% Blue," has excellent guitar work by Scott MacMillan. Belting out the words like the Maritimes' answer to Etta James, Rita sounds like a woman who's lived and lost when she admits, *"90% stoned and 10% blue, that's how I woke this morning."* But she doesn't give up: *"This old world, she's gonna keep on moving/This old girl, she's gonna keep on turning."*

"Here's to the People," a lively, music hall-style tune, is a barbed tribute to all the unsupportive people she's even encountered:

> *Here's to the people who don't celebrate you*
> *Here's to the people who don't tolerate you*
> *Here's to the other side of whatever side I'm on*
> *Here's to the people who think I'm wrong, wrong, wrong.*

"Stephen Foster Song" takes a nostalgic look at childhood, when the words to songs seemed bound to come true. The melody is slow and broad, gospel-like. MacNeil recalls how music enveloped her in its powerful magic.

> *The Stephen Foster book you sent me*
> *Brought back dreams of another century*
> *When I would climb upon the stool*
> *And try to play old Stephen's tunes.*

Her voice is wistful on the chorus: *"O Susannah, it'll never be the same again."* The dreams of an earlier time cannot be fulfilled, but still there is the joy of music.

I'm Not What I Seem is more poetic than MacNeil's previous albums. Her she uses words to paint pictures, not just express feelings. "Kwan Yin Doll" tells of a friend who grew up too fast, throwing away her innocence and youth in a cruel world. In writing this song Rita departed from her usual method. "I don't usually invent lives for other people," she says, "because no one really knows how another person feels." But in this case, compassion compelled her. "I sang it for my friend before I performed it, to make sure she understood what I was saying and felt comfortable with me making it public." She evokes the image of a *"Kwan Yin doll with her head bowed in mercy in your Victorian living room,"* then addresses the young woman: *"I remember when you were queen of the fashion world.../You were wise but not by years.../The price you had to pay is what you threw away."*

"I'm Not What I Seem," the album's most introspective song, takes MacNeil from adversity, through the process of becoming her own person, and finally to acceptance of herself.

> *I'm not what I seem and I'm not what you're seeing*
> *I'm a real creation of somebody's dream*
> *Somebody's nightmare, somebody's mistake*
> *But it all depends on who's doing the looking.*

"This was one of the first songs I wrote, but I didn't record it until much later," Rita says. "What I meant was, when you're out there singing people expect you to look a certain way, to fit in. Well, I don't fit in. One way is my size. Some people might see me and think, 'Can you imagine looking like her?' I wrote the song from that perspective. 'Who's doing the looking' is the hook line. I'm not bothered by people's reactions 'cause it's their problem, not mine."

I'm Not What I Seem was MacNeil's most successful album at the time, selling about 15,000 copies. During the summers of 1983 and '84 she appeared at the Vancouver, Winnipeg and Mariposa Folk Festivals and mader her first cross-Canada tour in 1985. The Canadian media finally began to notice. Newspapers wrote about the shy woman from Big Pond with the black fedora and splendid voice. She played larger halls with more broadly-based audiences. Richard Flohil, a Toronto manager and promoter, says, "Rita began to make a real audience crossover. Her crowds were no longer just feminists or Maritimers, but a mixture of people: old, young and middle aged, middle class, male and female, gay and straight, folk, country and rock fans." For the first time she began to make a modest living from her records and concerts.

1983. In the early days, Rita and Joella jokingly invented outrageous goals — crazy, impossible goals, like selling out the Rebecca Cohn Auditorium in Halifax. Now MacNeil is waiting in the wings of that hall, ready to sing — to a sold out house. She paces, reaching up to touch her black fedora, folding her hands, unfolding them, taking off the hat, smoothing her hair, putting the hat back on.

She stops. "I can't go out there."

Her band gathers round. Joella puts her arm around Rita's shoulders. "It's OK, Rita."

MacNeil shakes her head. "I can't — "

"Yes, you can," says Ralph. "You'll be fine."

The band forms a huddle, arms across each other's backs.

"You can do it, Rita."

"They just want to hear you sing."

"But — "

"And now, from Big Pond, Cape Breton, Rita MacNeil," the announcer's voice booms. The applause beings.

The band members give Rita a group hug. "Break a leg," Joella whispers, nudging her toward the stage.

MacNeil hesitates at the curtain. She takes a deep breath, then steps onstage. The applause grows louder. With a nod and a smile to the audience, she kicks off her shoes and starts to sing.

By 1985, Ralph Dillon was still arranging Rita's songs, playing keyboards and leading the band, but he felt he could not also manage her career. He asked Brookes Diamond, a Halifax-based music promoter, to take over. Diamond felt that MacNeil was being under-booked, under-paid, and under-appreciated. "Everywhere I inquired, people told me that Rita was a star waiting for a place to happen," he says. He booked her into better clubs, improved the routing so she had to travel less, got her more work, made sure the lights and sound were taken care of, and arranged publicity. He freed Rita and her band to concentrate on the music.

In 1985 she played at EXPO 85 in Osaka, Japan. As well she was profiled on CBC Radio's "Sunday Morning" and on TV's "The Journal." But perhaps the biggest breakthrough came when she performed for five weeks at EXPO 86 in Vancouver, the longest-running stint at the fair. According to Brookes Diamond, "Rita had never had a chance to go into a large centre and get exposure to thousands of people. She was one of the most successful artists at the festival. The West, especially British Columbia, became a base of support for her."

After EXPO, MacNeil's career really took off. Newspaper articles praised her singing and songwriting. She was featured on radio and TV. Almost as soon as she returned home, she went into the recording studio. *Flying On Your Own*, released late in 1986 on the Lupins Records label, coincided with her rising popularity and made her the star that so many people had predicted she would someday become.

1986. On a sunny spring day, MacNeil is driving from Cape Breton to Halifax. This is no ordinary trip. It's the first time she's driven this route alone. Always before she's depended on buses, friends or

*relatives to drive her. But recently, feeling more independent — and
more solvent — she's bought a car.*

*Humming a new melody, she approaches the toll bridge linking
Dartmouth to Halifax. She feels proud and confident. Her quarter
is ready. At the toll gate she rolls down her window and throws the
coin at the basket. She misses. The light stays red. A siren blares.
Rita panics, presses the gas pedal to the floor and speeds away.*

*After calming down, Rita begins to think about all the ways she's
doing more for herself now, depending on others less. The thoughts
become lyrics. Several months later, "Flying On Your Own" becomes
a hit all across Canada.*

Her aim improves.

Flying On Your Own was produced differently from MacNeil's
earlier albums. For one thing, she had more control over the production. "She had little to do with making her first three records,"
Brookes Diamond says. "She was too shy to get involved. But on
Flying On Your Own she had a lot to do with the sound."

Some of the songs were produced with a conscious goal: "We
attempted to make Rita's music more compatible with radio by
using more pop arrangements," Diamond explains. To this end,
MacNeil worked with Declan O'Doherty, who produced the title
track and "Fast Train to Tokyo" in Nashville, using studio musicians. The rest were produced by Ralph Dillon in Canada.
"Declan is a gentle man," Brookes says. "He worked well with
Rita. He took 'Flying' and put a sound around it that fit with radio
programming." That sound is more sophisticated than much of
MacNeil's earlier music, with more synthesizers and layered
instrumentals.

The pop tune "Neon City," set in Toronto, portrays the effects
of the fast urban life on relationships:

> *Oh that Neon City, where the lights warm up the night
> And lovers become strangers and strangers become lost.*

The voice of hindsight looks back with regret:

> *If you could hold me now like you held me then
> We'd be two less lonely people trying to forget.*

Tinkling, staccato notes on the synthesizer simulate rain falling on
cold city streets and provide an eerie contrast to the warmth of
Rita's voice.

The familiar theme of home, harkening back to *Part of the
Mystery*, appears in two songs. Rita composed "She's Called Nova
Scotia" while in Vancouver for EXPO 86. "I was homesick and I
wanted to share my love for Nova Scotia with the people of British

Columbia." After a haunting flute introduction, she sings slowly and sweetly:

> *Walk through her green fields, go down to the sea*
> *The fortune in your eyes is more like a dream*
> *She's called Nova Scotia and she so makes you feel*
> *You'll discover a treasure no other has seen.*

"Realized Your Dreams" is a tribute to a Big Pond resident who found happiness and wisdom living a quiet life in the place of his birth, while others searched for fulfillment in busy cities and exotic places. "When I and many others were leaving, he never left," Rita says, her face lighting up at the thought of him. "He's so marvelous and secure. You get the feeling he's been everywhere even though he's never been anywhere."

> *It's the drifter and the dreamer who often fail to see*
> *In the heart that never wanders lies a peace that comes with morning*
> *It's knowing when the day is done you've realized your dreams.*

In "Fast Train to Tokyo," inspired by Rita's visit to Japan in 1985, people reach out and touch one another, then pass out of each other's lives. The song is addressed, as are most of MacNeil's tunes, to a "you"—a lover, perhaps, or an acquaintance, but it moves beyond personal relationships to a universal viewpoint:

> *I believe we're all part of the tempest*
> *That moves our lives in different directions*
> *We pass on, we pass on.*

The Oriental-sounding synthesizer refrain creates a mysterious atmosphere, against which a fast, light drumbeat suggests the relentless motion of crossing lives.

The title track is the record's masterpiece. "'Flying On Your Own' is the key song that sums up everything I've done and everything I hope will come," MacNeil says. The song encapsulates her life and her music—from hard times to success, from confusion to self-discovery, from doubt to confidence and hope. Against a synthesizer-led background, her voice soars:

> *When you know the wings you ride*
> *That keep you in the sky*
> *There isn't anyone holding back you.*
>
> *First you stumble, then you fall*
> *You reach out and you fly*
> *There isn't anything you can't do.*

Flying On Your Own has been phenomenally successful. In the *Chronicle-Herald/Mail-Star*, Stephen Pedersen said, "It's a brilliant album...a summing up of the essential Rita, its eleven songs crossing the borders of folk, country and rock, all unified by Rita's unique sense of caring." By late 1987 the record had sold over 100,000 copies, exceeding by seven times the sales of *I'm Not What I Seem*. MacNeil was catapulted into the sphere of Canadian stardom. Her Juno award only made official what tens of thousands of Canadians already knew.

"Rita is a fabulous entertainer," Brookes Diamond says. "She makes people laugh, she makes them cry. She sings beautiful songs to them and they go home feeling wonderful." But for MacNeil, performing remains a challenge. "I still get nervous and excited. Stepping out on stage isn't any easier." She describes herself as an intensely shy person, saying, "If you put me in a party I'll probably seek the nearest corner." Yet onstage she appears natural and relaxed, sharing self-deprecating anecdotes with the audience in her soft brogue. Partly she has conquered her shyness through the use of a talisman, her hat, without which she feels vulnerable. And partly, as she puts it, "My belief in my music has helped me persevere and face the stage." Once in front of the spotlights, she relaxes. "It's as if there's two people—the one that's on the stage and the one that isn't. When I'm up there I feel a reaching out and a drawing in. I feel at home." She pauses, then adds, "Maybe it's easier to open your heart from up there."

The recent fame leaves Rita surprised, delighted and awed. "Sometimes I have the feeling it's all happening to someone else," she says with a shy smile. "When I started to get acceptance and recognition for my music a few years ago, it felt strange because I hadn't approached my career with that as an aim. I'd always wanted to sing and I had an inner need to express myself. That's why I became a musician. What's happened is wonderful and unbelievable."

But success brings drawbacks: increased demands on her time, more probing into her life, less chance to enjoy the tranquility of Big Pond, more traveling and time away from her children (her daughter attends university in Halifax, and her son, a recent high school graduate and aspiring musician, lives with her in Sydney). Because of her busy schedule, she now writes more on the road than at home. "Sometimes it's scary and I can't believe all the hype—or I don't want to believe it." Still, she appreciates people's acceptance of her and her music. When she flew into Halifax after receiving the Juno award, the entire community of Big Pond was at the airport to greet her with flowers and banners, and her new neighbours in Sydney, where she has bought a house, placed a huge bouquet on her doorstep. "It's like I'm their daughter," she says with quiet satisfaction.

1987. Rita MacNeil walks onstage at the National Arts Centre in Ottawa. Even before she opens her mouth to sing, the audience erupts in applause, whistles and cheers. She smiles her shy smile. "Thank you," she says, and again, "Thank you." As if rescuing her, the band launches into the first number. She kicks off her shoes and starts to sway. Her voice fills the hall, reaching the corners of the building and the corners of people's hearts with songs about love and loss, hard times and fun, her island home. She is called back for four encores. Finally, as the band plays "Stephen Foster Song," the girl who wanted to be a singer bows one last time and leaves the stage.

Discography

Heather Bishop — all on Mother of Pearl Records
Grandmother's Song — 1979
Celebration — 1981
I Love Women Who Laugh — 1982
A Taste of the Blues — 1987
Bellybutton — 1982
Purple People Eater — 1985

Ferron — all on Lucy Records
Ferron — 1977
Ferron Backed Up — 1978   out of print
Testimony — 1980
Shadows on a Dime — 1984

Marie-Lynn Hammond (solo records) — all on Black Tie Records
Marie-Lynn Hammond — 1979
Vignettes — 1983
Impromptu — 1985 (cassette only)

Connie Kaldor
One Of These Days — 1981
Moonlight Grocery — 1984   Coyote Records
New Songs for an Old Celebration (with Roy Forbes) —
    Festival Records — 1986

Rita MacNeil
Born A Woman — Boot Records — 1975
Part of the Mystery — Big Pond Publishing and Production —
    1981
I'm Not What I Seem — World Records for University College
    of Cape Breton — 1983
Flying On Your Own — Lupins Records — 1986

Lucie Blue Tremblay

Lucie Blue Tremblay — Olivia Records — 1986

Sylvia Tyson (solo records)

Sylvia Tyson — Capitol Records — 1975
Woman's World — Capitol Records — 1977
Satin on Stone — Salt Records — 1978
Sugar for Sugar, Salt for Salt — Salt Records — 1979
Big Spotlight — Stony Plain Records — 1986 (cassette only)